Tamarack & Clearcut

Haiku by Marianne Bluger
Photographs by Rudi Haas

CARLETON UNIVERSITY PRESS

Tamarack & Clearcut

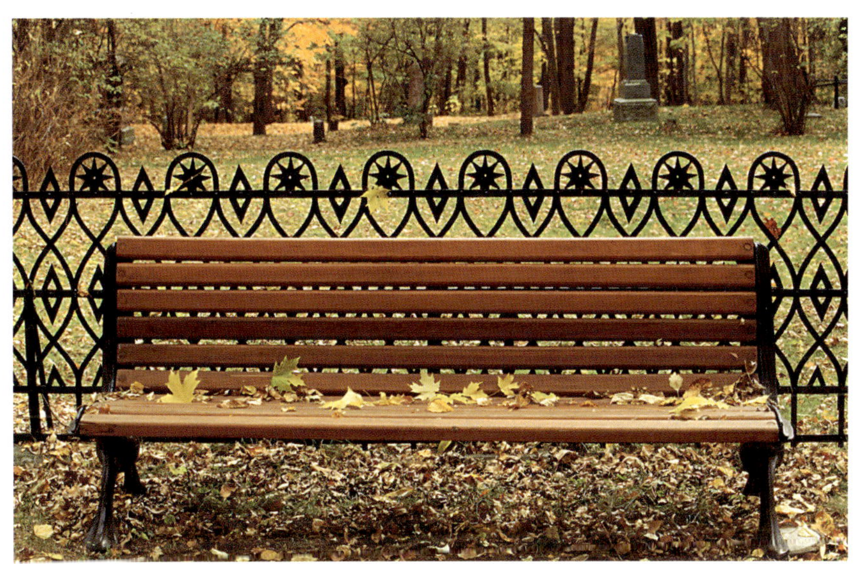

Haiku by Marianne Bluger
Photographs by Rudi Haas

CARLETON UNIVERSITY PRESS

Canadian Cataloguing in Publication Data

Bluger, Marianne
Tamarack and clearcut : haiku

ISBN 0-88629-293-X

I. Haas, Rudi II. Title

PS8553.L85T34 1996 C813'.54 C96-901035-4
PR9199.3.B555T34 1996

Carleton University Press gratefully acknowledges the support extended to its publishing program by the Canada Council for the Arts, and the Ontario Arts Council. The Publisher would also like thank the Department of Canadian Heritage, Government of Canada, and the Government of Ontario through the Ministry of Culture, Tourism and Recreation, for their assistance. The Publisher also acknowledges the generosity of Dr. Naomi Jackson Groves, whose enthusiasm inspired the convergence of Marianne Bluger's haiku and Rudi Haas's photographs.

Cover design: Your Aunt Nellie
Interior design: Carl Crew

Printed in Canada by M.O.M. Printing

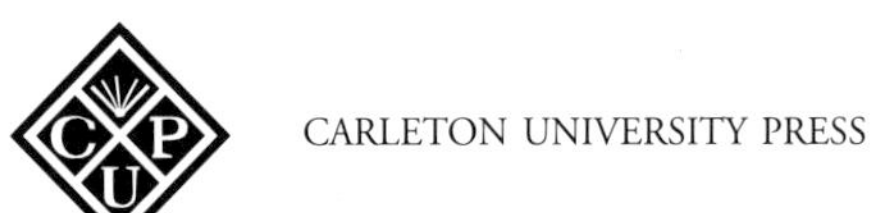

CARLETON UNIVERSITY PRESS

Born in Ottawa, MARIANNE BLUGER is a lyric poet who for twenty years has practised the old Japanese discipline of writing haiku. Her haiku, like her lyrics, exhibit a grounded vision expressed with such charm that Louis Dudek has written of her work, "It's a superb collection. I'm absolutley floored, delighted, enthralled."

A passionate naturalist, Bluger is well matched in this collaboration with Rudi Haas, another Ottawan, whose instinctive grasp of the power of the natural image complements her own.

Marianne Bluger gratefully acknowledges the Ontario Arts Council and the Regional Municipality of Ottawa-Carleton for grants to write poetry included in this book. Some of these poems first appeared in Japan, in *Azami, Mainichi Daily News, New Cicada, and Oku no Hosomichi*; in the United States, in *Brussels Sprout, Dragonfly, Frogpond, Haiku Southwest, Modern Haiku, Wind Chimes*; and in Canada, in *The Alchemist, Anthologie de haiku d'auteurs canadiens, Cicada, Haiku Canada Society Anthologies 1987-92, Haiku Canada Newsletter, Inkstone, Milkweed, Raw Nervz, Tidepool,* and *Tree.* Some poems were also published in the broadsheets: *April &, The Marigolds, & is the Hub*; and in *Haiku Moment* (Tuttle), and *Summer Grass* (Brick Books), which won the Archibald Lampman Award.

Thanks to Rod Willmot, Larry Neily, Ikkoku Santo, Dorothy Howard and George Johnston for useful comments on some of the poems. The poet acknowledges with thanks the help of Rudi Haas, Hans Blohm, Barbara Cumming and John Flood.

Marianne Bluger dedicates this book to Maji, Agi, and to Larry.

A former recipient of the Art Directors Gold Medal Award, RUDI HAAS is well known as co-author of the *Egg Carton Zoo* books and of *Ottawa: Our Nation's Capital.* As a graphic designer he has a wealth of experience with both commercial and creative productions. Representing the latter, the work in the present publication demonstrates the acute sensitivity of the photographer's sense of place.

The photographs in *Tamarack & Clearcut* are all taken in and around Ottawa. For Haas, they do not require captions, or descriptions, or commentary about his camera-work. Instead, they stand as miniature revelations about a photographer's fascination with his ever-changing surroundings. Born in Austria in the mid 1930s, Rudi Haas includes among his influences the work of Hokusai, Matisse, Goya, Klimt, Cartier-Bresson, Bischoph, and the Canadian artist Christiane Pflug. Haas writes:

"In the middle of a successful career, my health collapsed after a tropical fever in 1971, and I had to give up all attempts at purposeful occupation. In the past two years, however, thanks to the perceptiveness and encouragement of other people involved in this project, I have begun to recapture the immediacy that used to distinguish my earlier work. There was the challenge of a fine poet like Marianne Bluger — whose work is so different and, in many ways, so much the same that our work can stand side by side, perhaps as spontaneous juxtaposition; and of great friends such as Hans and Ingeborg Blohm — whose perseverance has been so inspiring and unselfish."

Thanks also to Michael Ashiq, Paul and Marie von Baich, Ken J. Brown, Ginger Kelly, Maisa Lilja, Kelly O'Gorman, Mairuth and Dominick Sarsfield, and Anne de Shield-Packwood. Rudi Haas dedicates his part of this book to Naomi Jackson Groves.

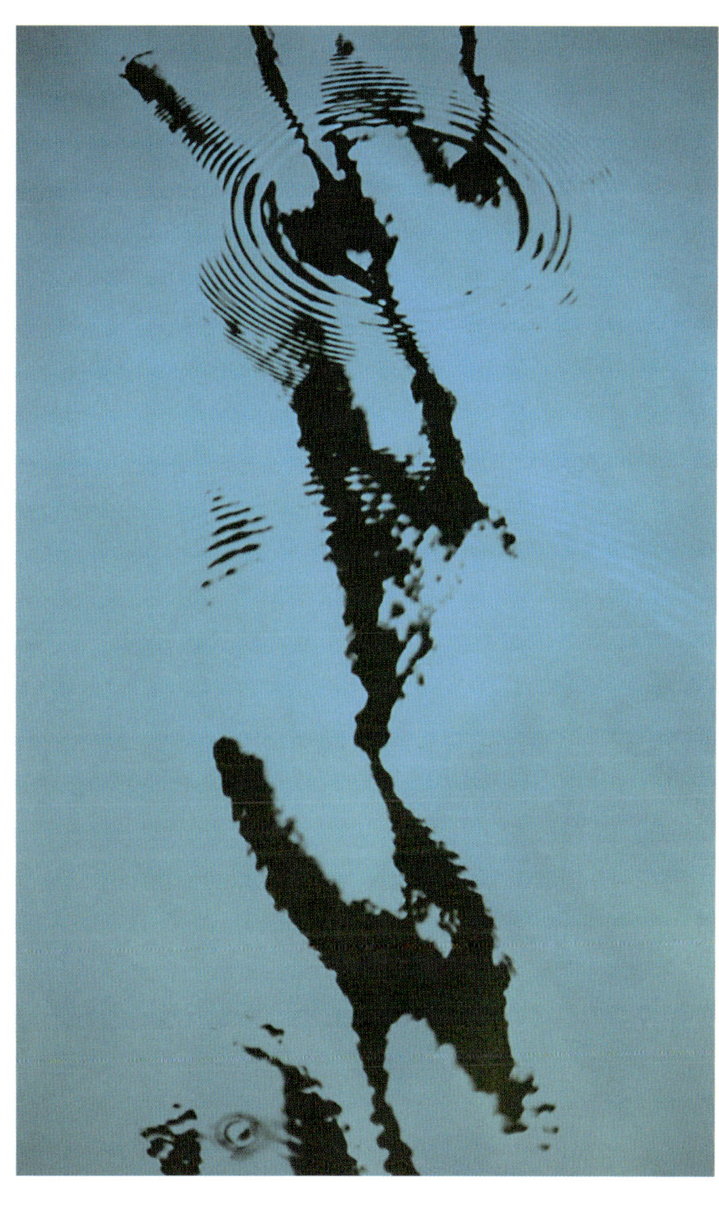

Leafsmoke

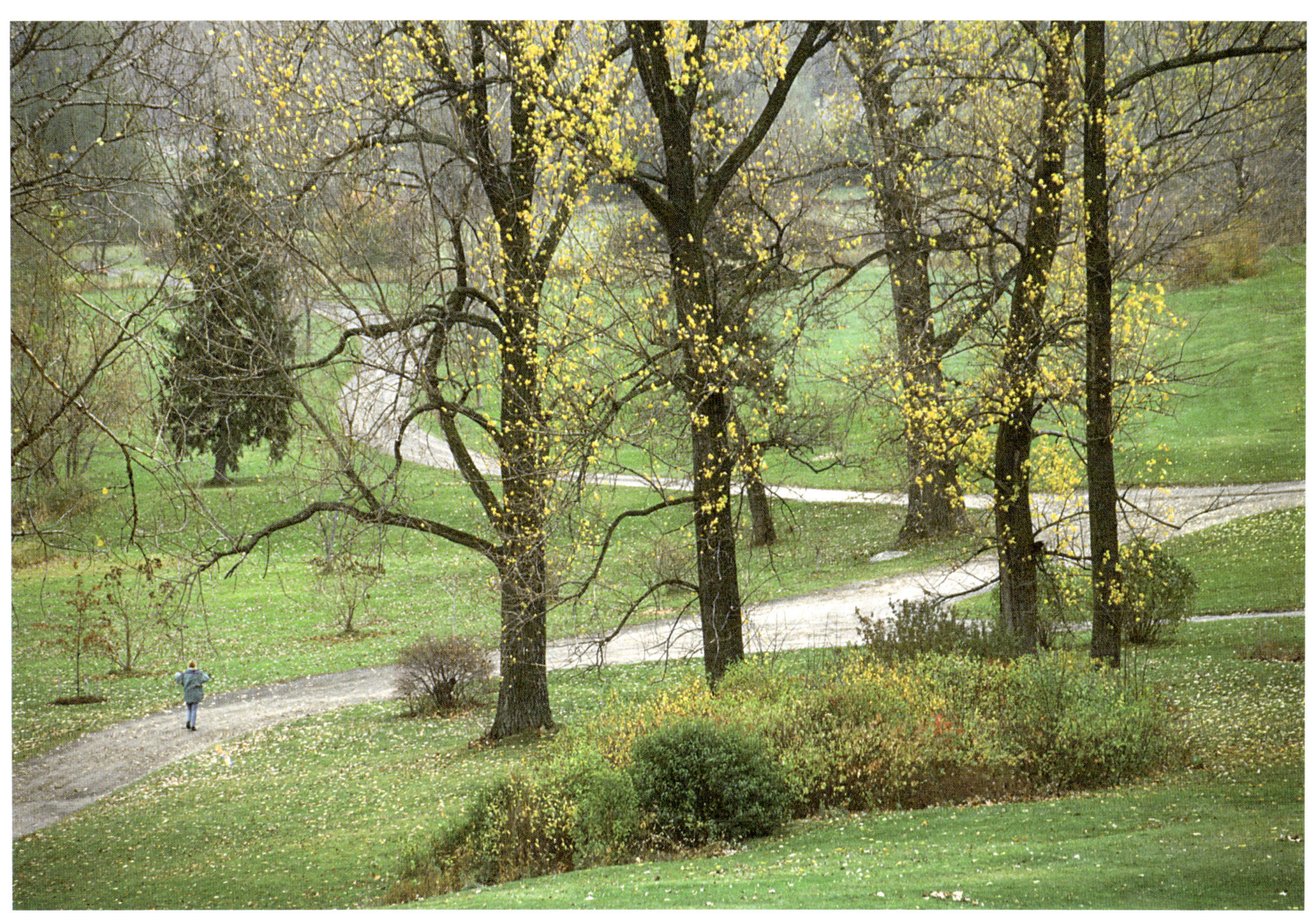

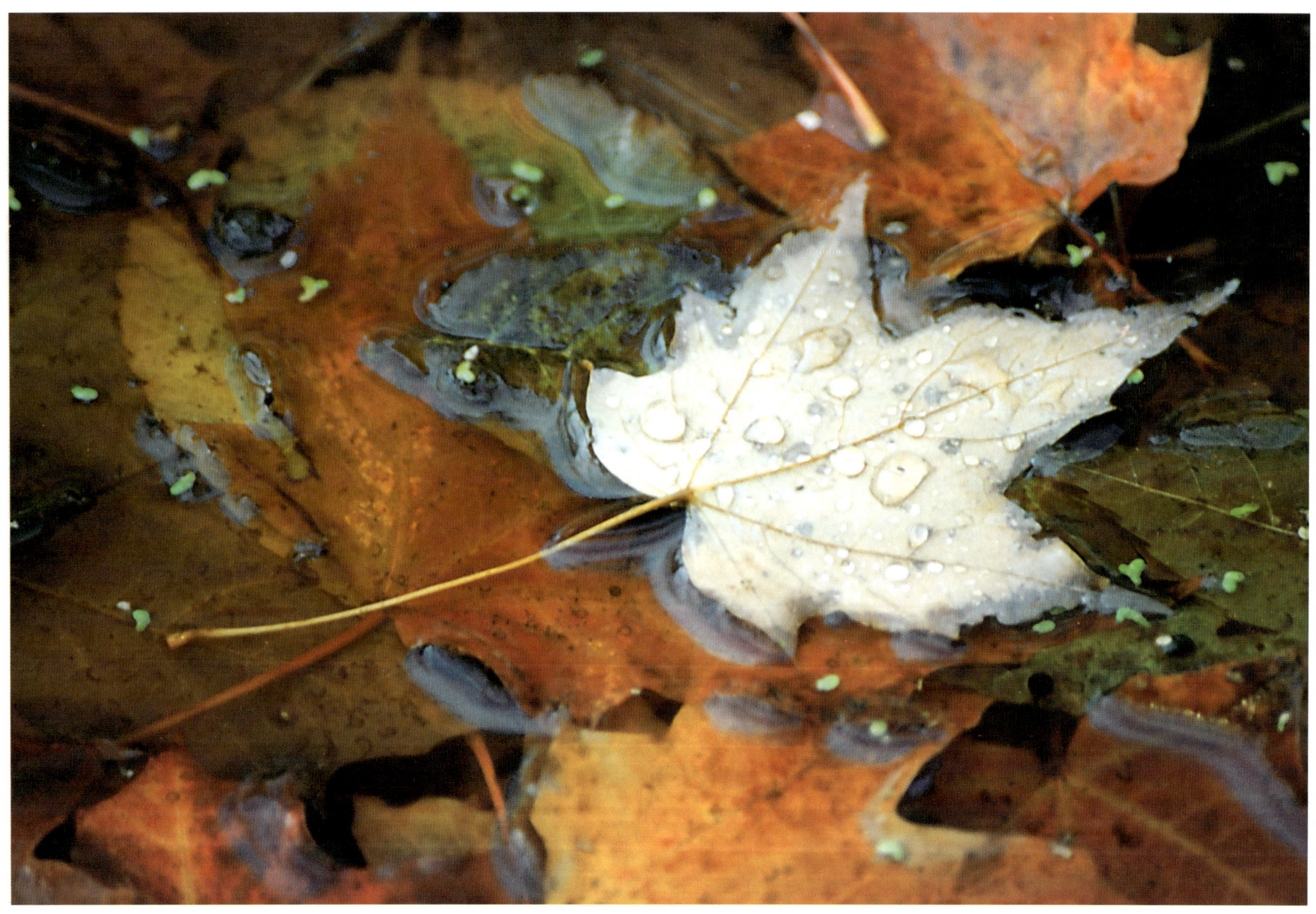

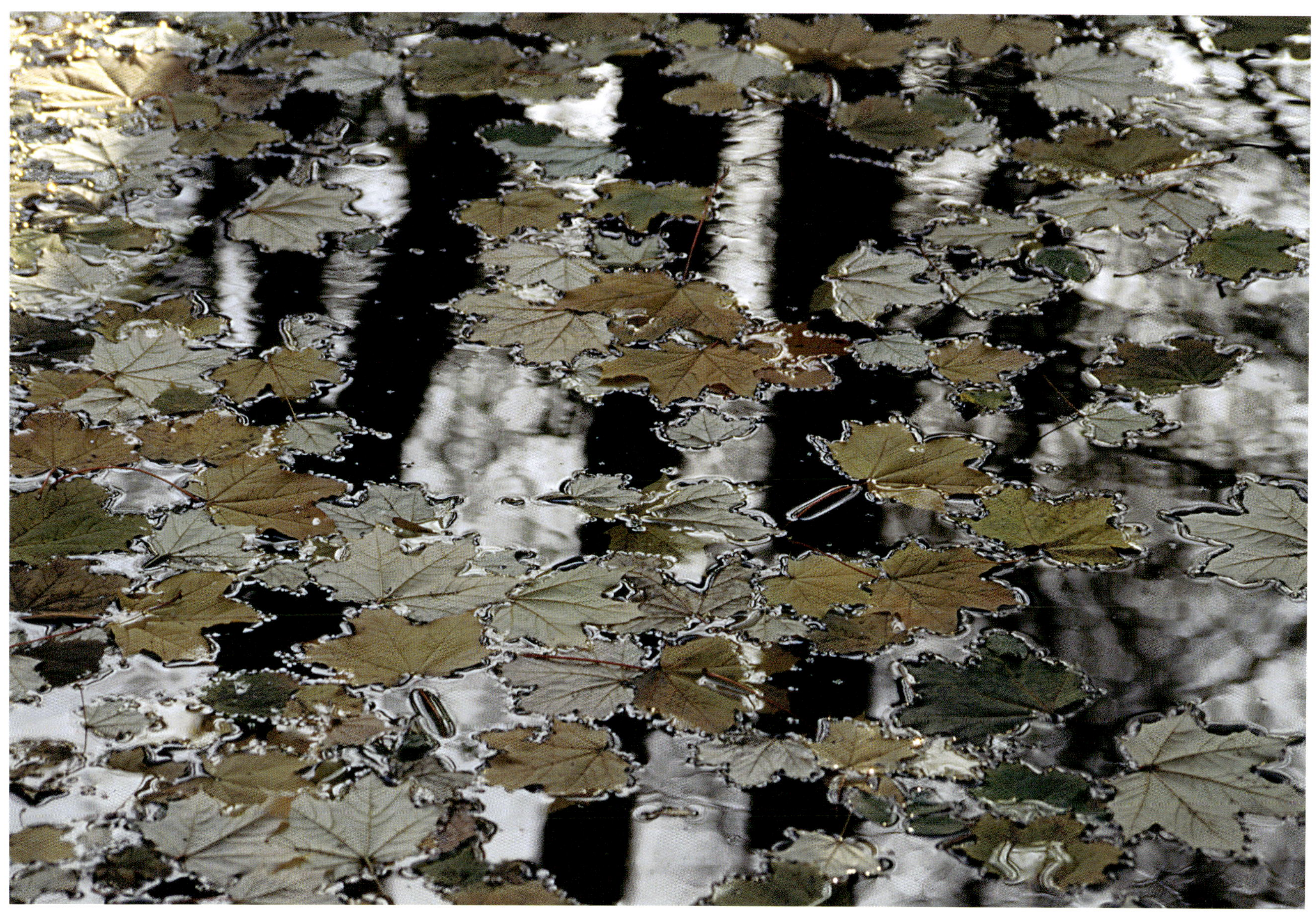

end of the season
upwind on cold sand
a gull struts

a scorched smell —
burnt fields in the rain
the boulders steam

in a dark window
Dad's pale face
watching our bonfire soar

fogbound
in a hotel room
reruns ...

swallows
skirling in the indigo canyon
— or blowing leaves ...

darkness
moving in among the pines
a screen door slams

a drifting leaf
& I — in another life
a Zen master's wife

car-sound fading
on the clear mountain air —
gasoline

on the mountain lake
a pier in silence floats
on empty oildrums

wind bunts
the marigolds
bunt back

mad shadows
— a moth at the porchlight —
I grip a cold key

bared to sky now
abandoned
the nest of a hawk

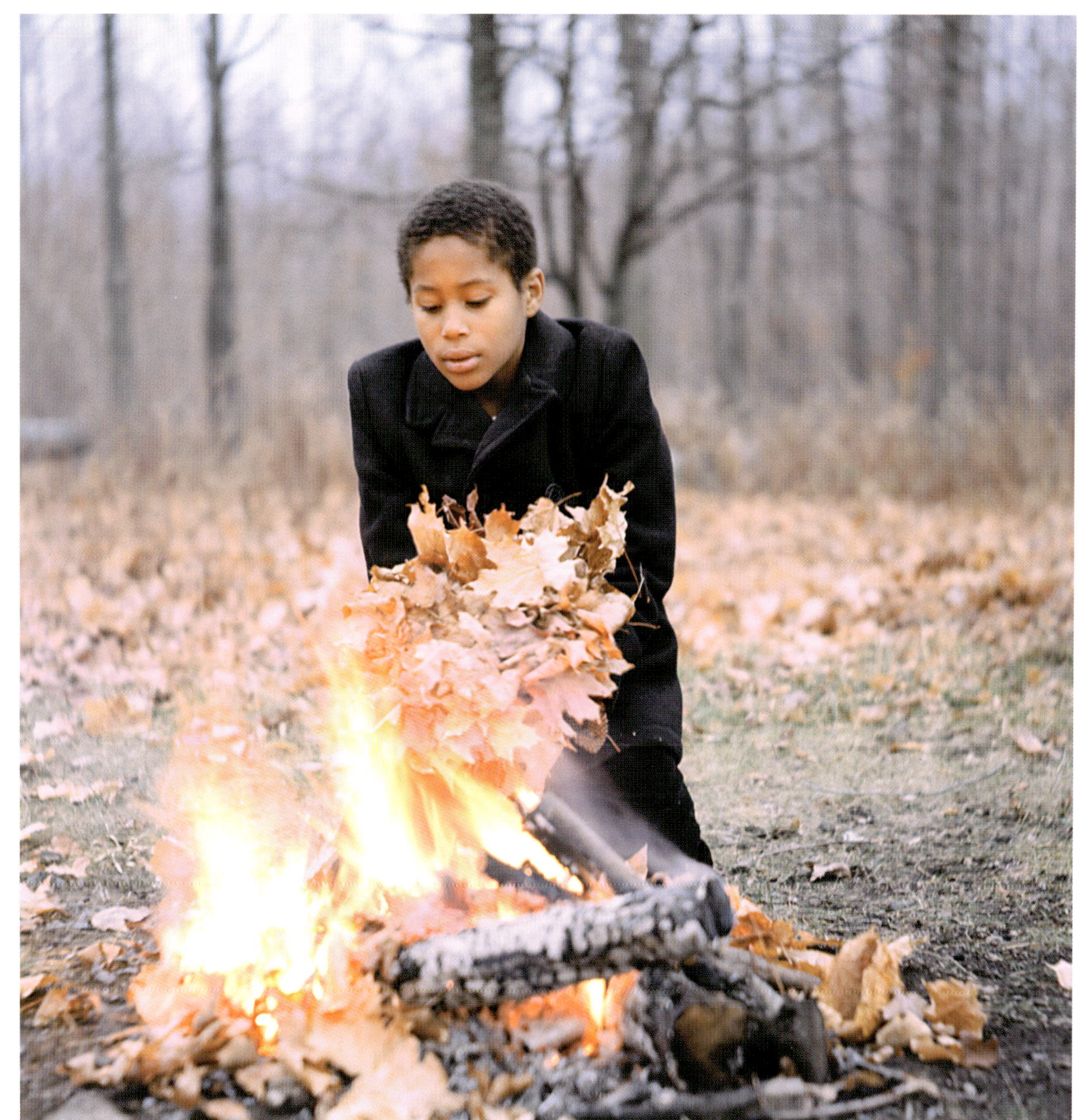

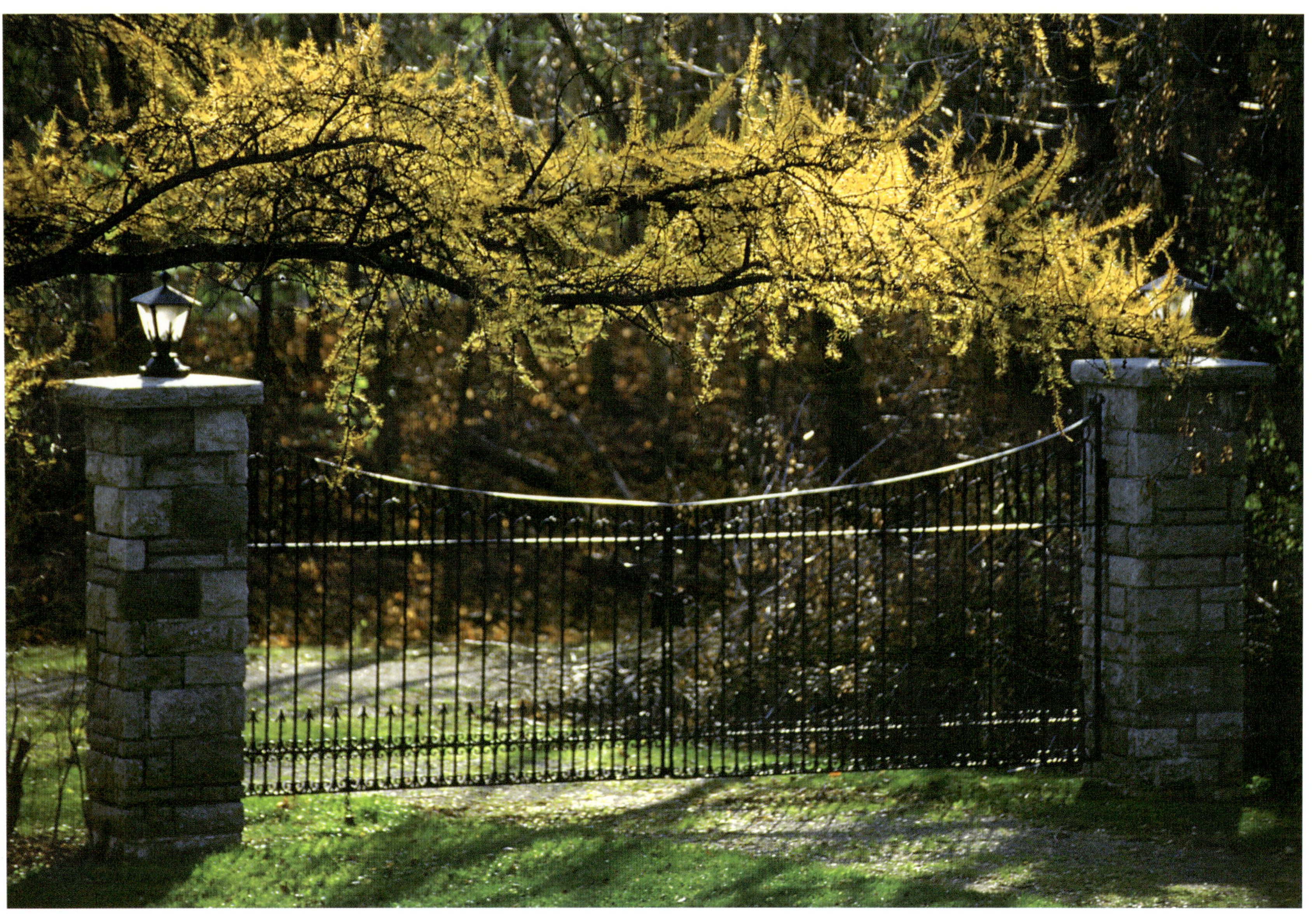

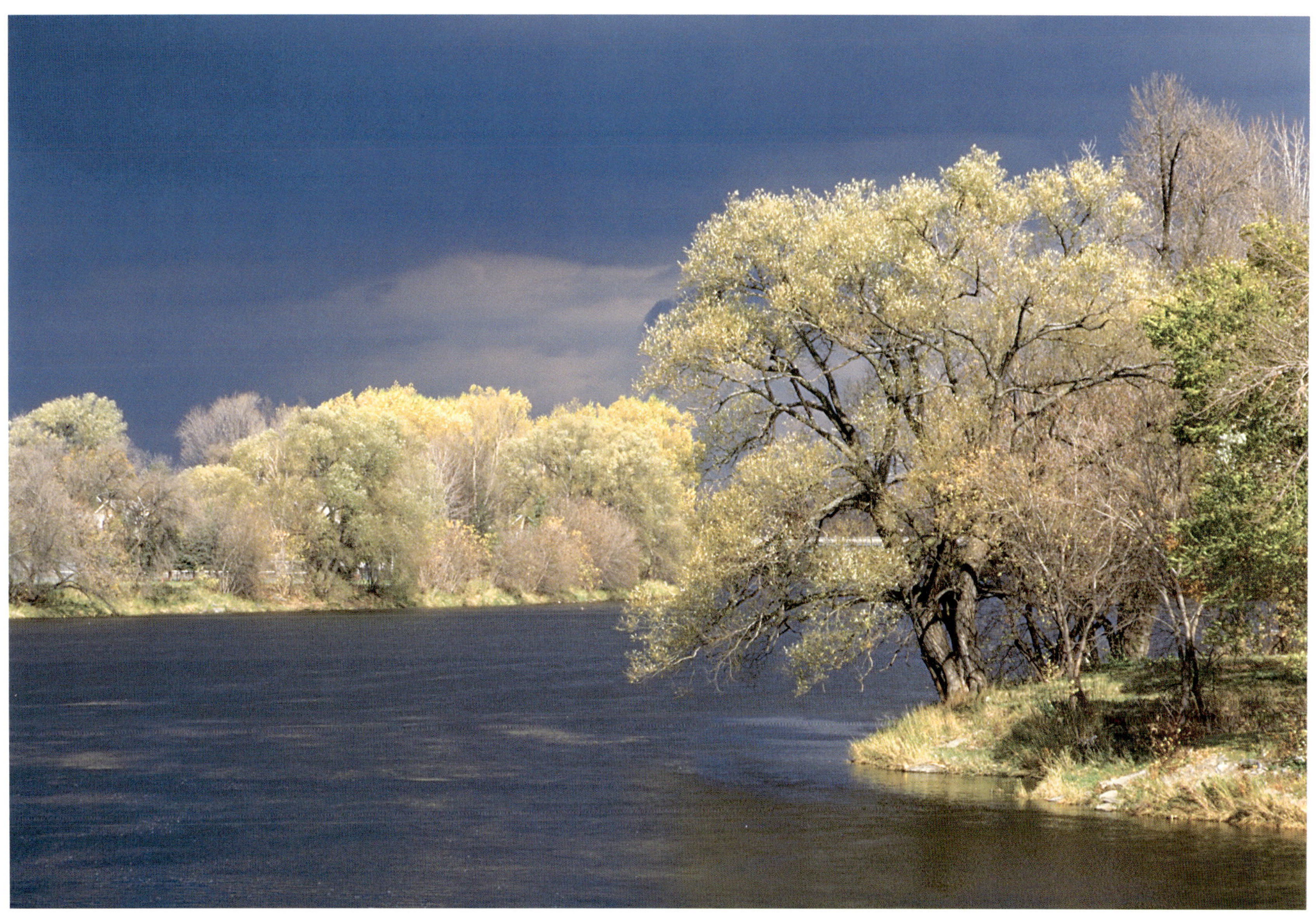

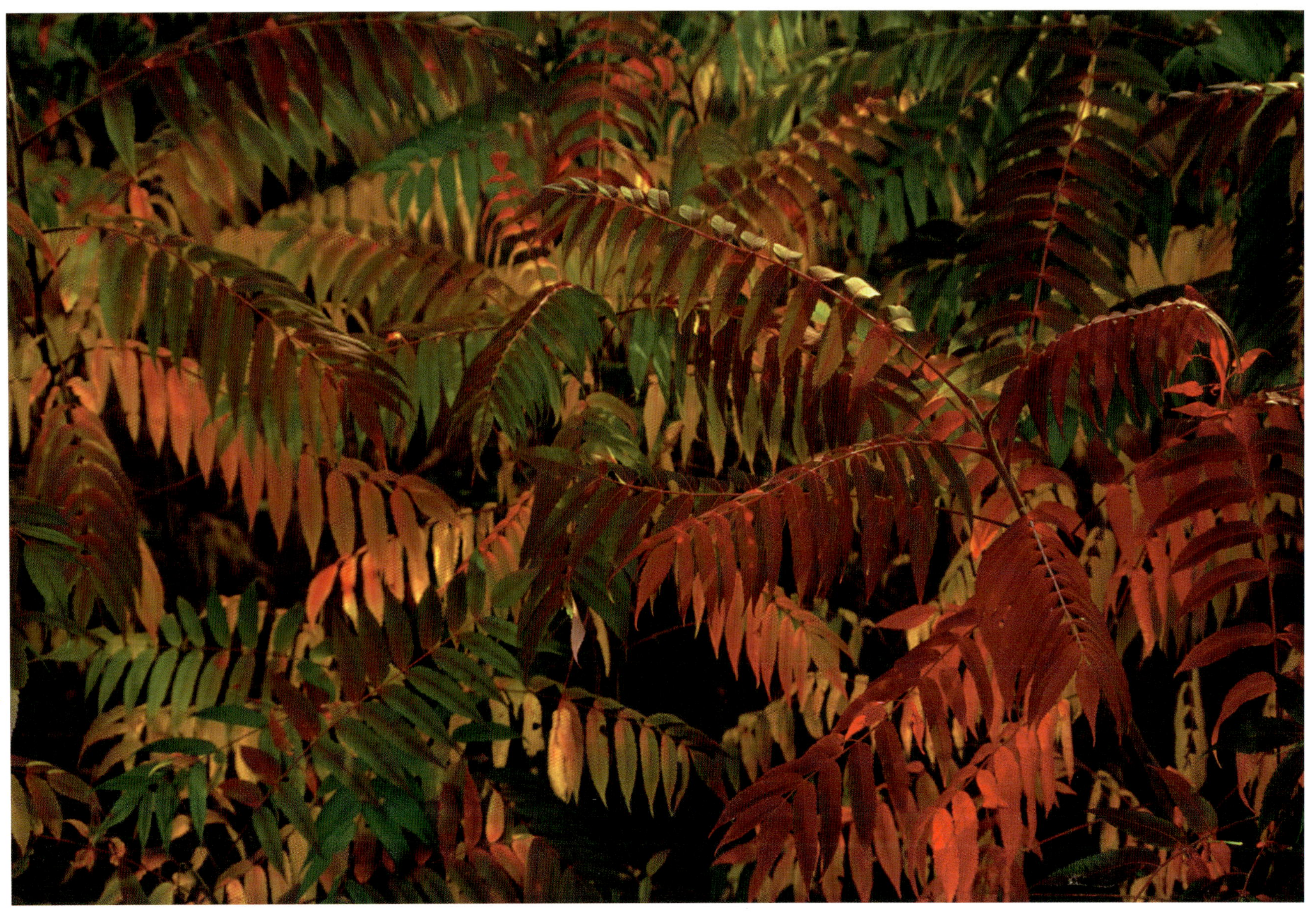

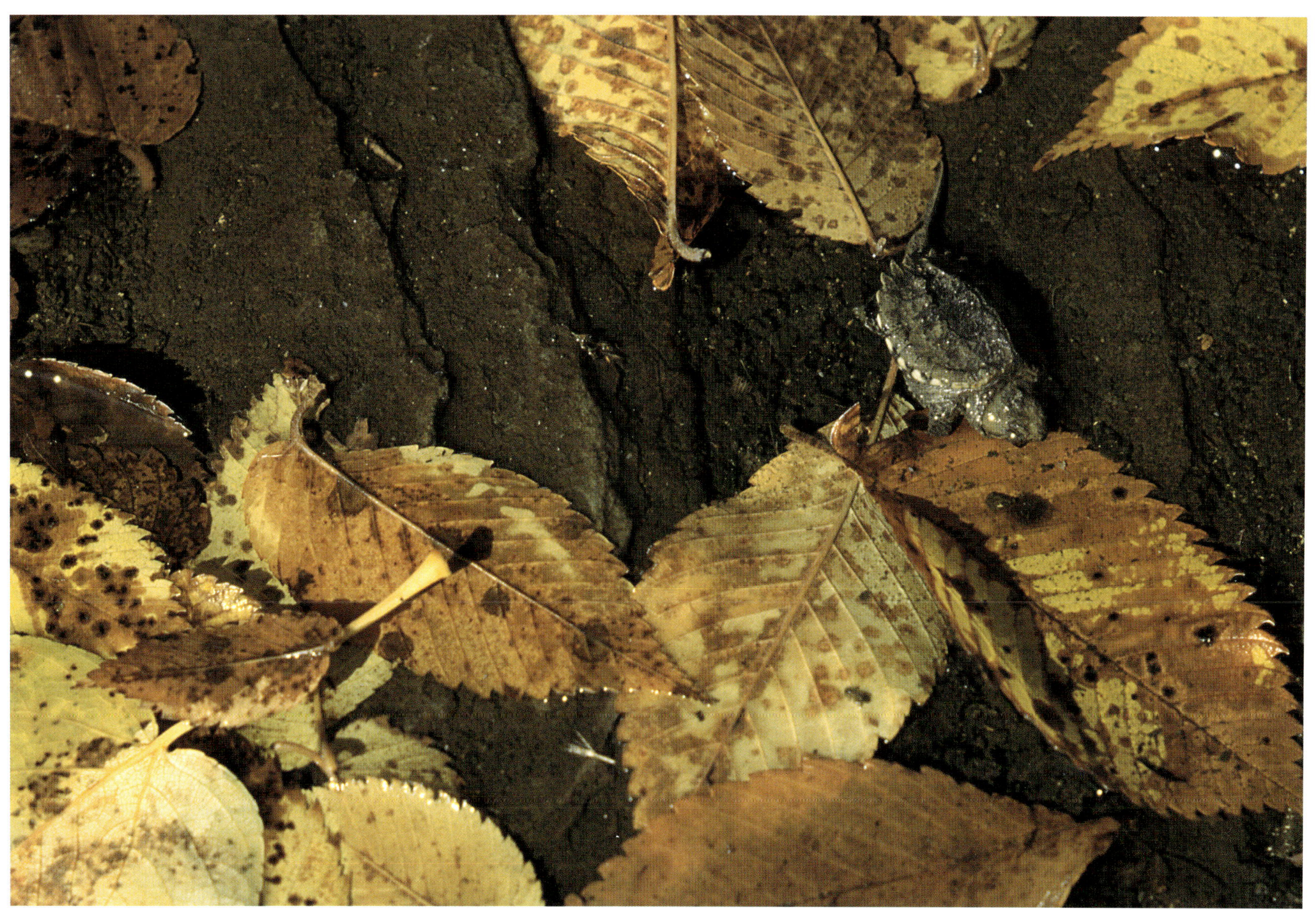

waves
as we argue
keep rolling

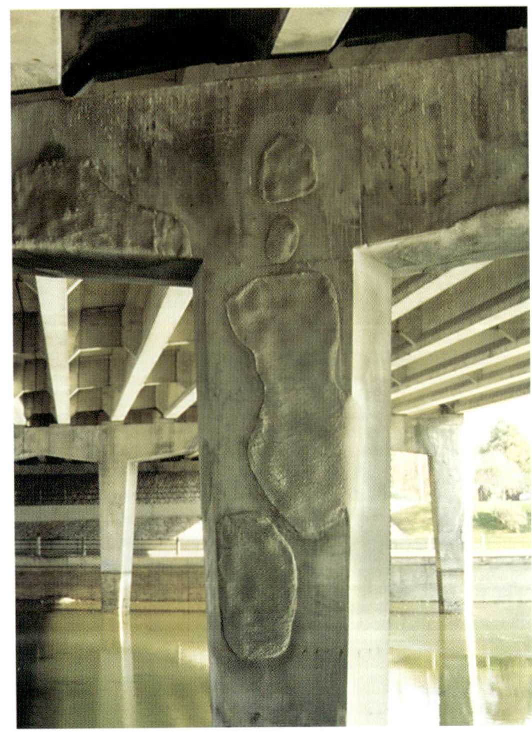

empty street
the last brown leaves
let go

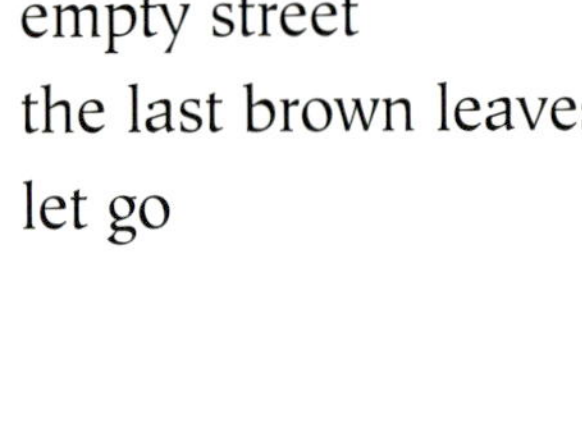

a maple key
spiralling into the gorge
where a Chevy rusts

evening falls
through his drowned grove
a beaver glides

cars flashing
up the Gatineau — highway
into sunset

slashing
the granite — scarlet
sumac

dazed with cold
a bumblebee clings
to a faded aster

bald from chemo
my friend Diana
a laughing Buddha

'for sale'
and wind
in the empty barn

among rusting girders
night fog drifts —
the bridge to Québec

this rainy night
out wandering anywhere
the wet leaves point

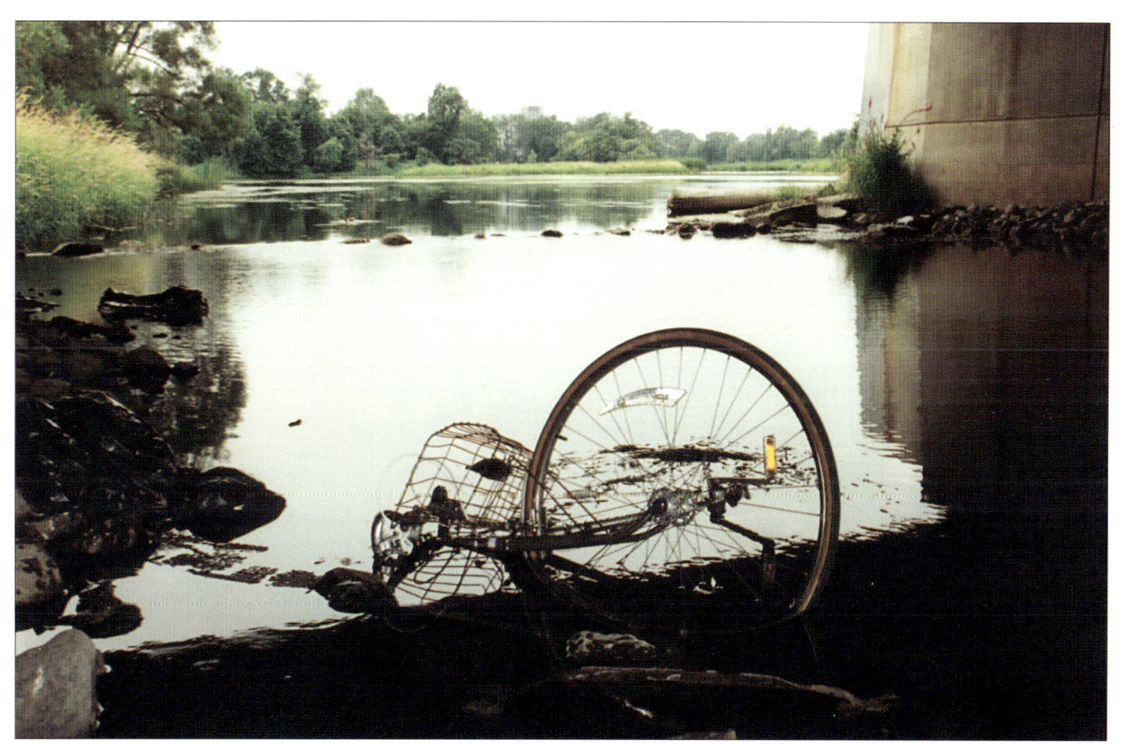

catching my skirt
wind scatters the crumbs
& sparrows ...

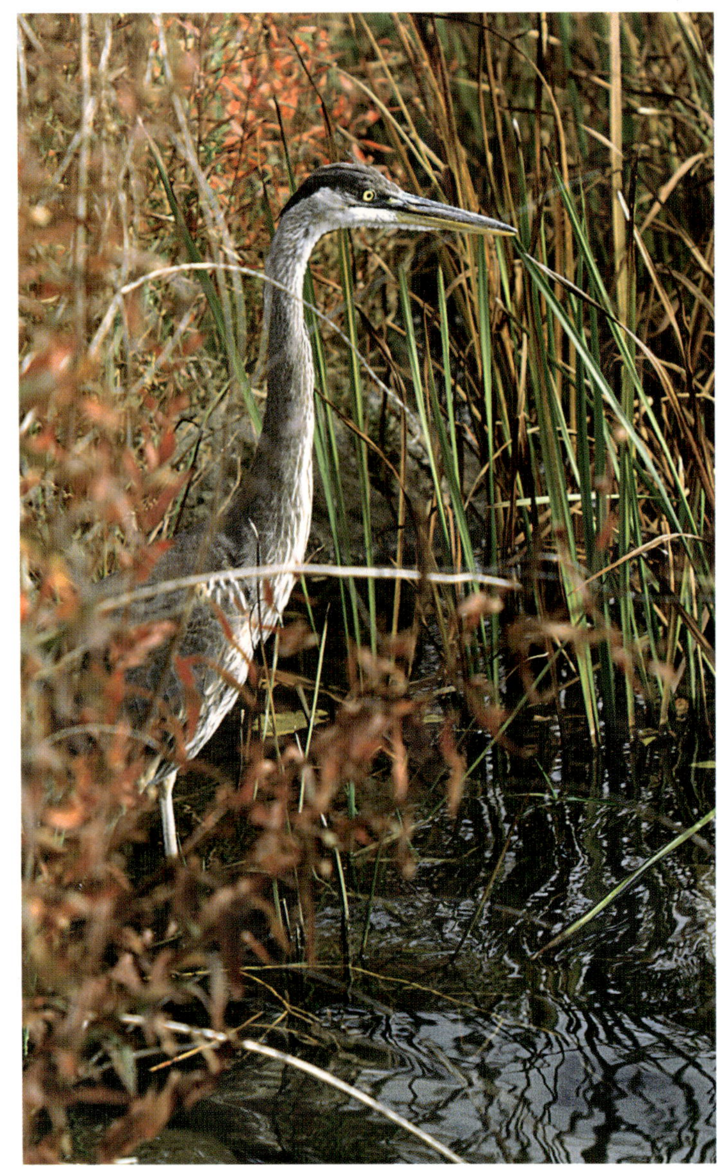

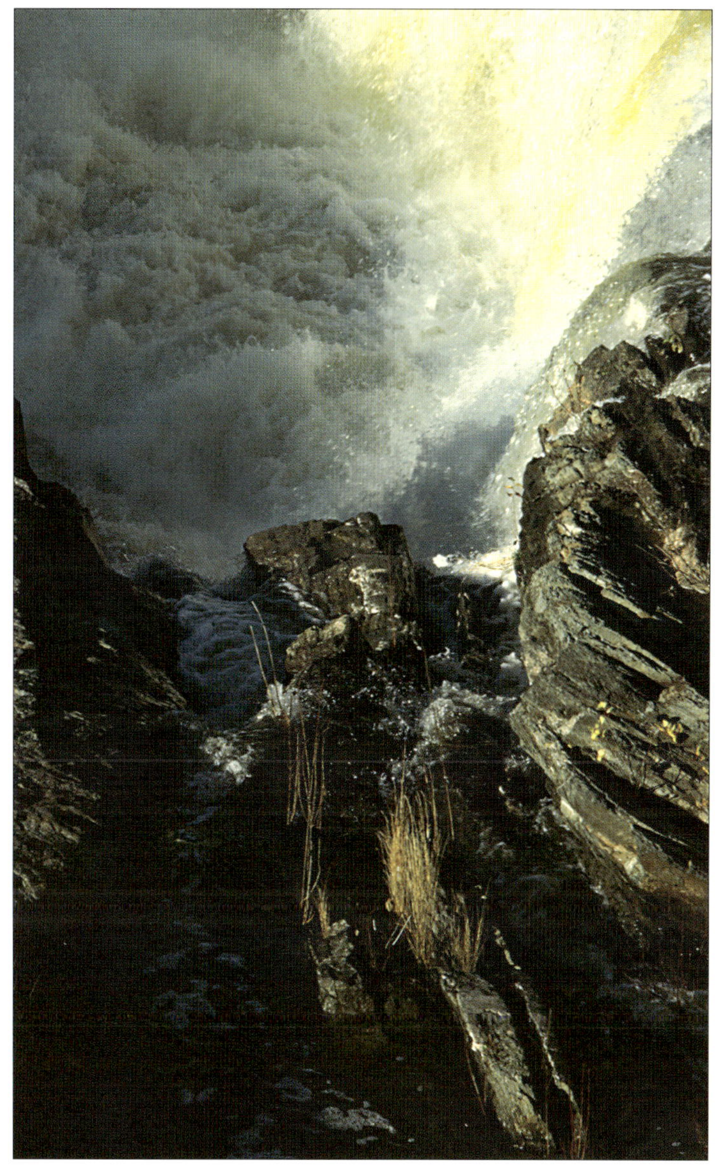

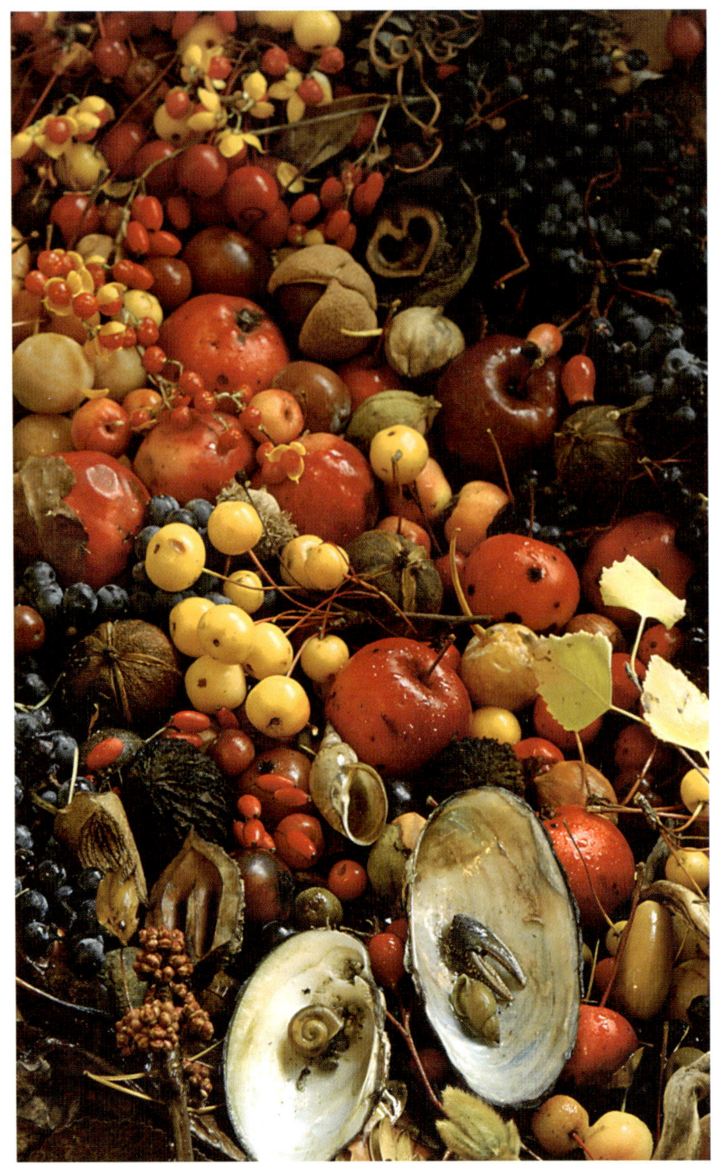

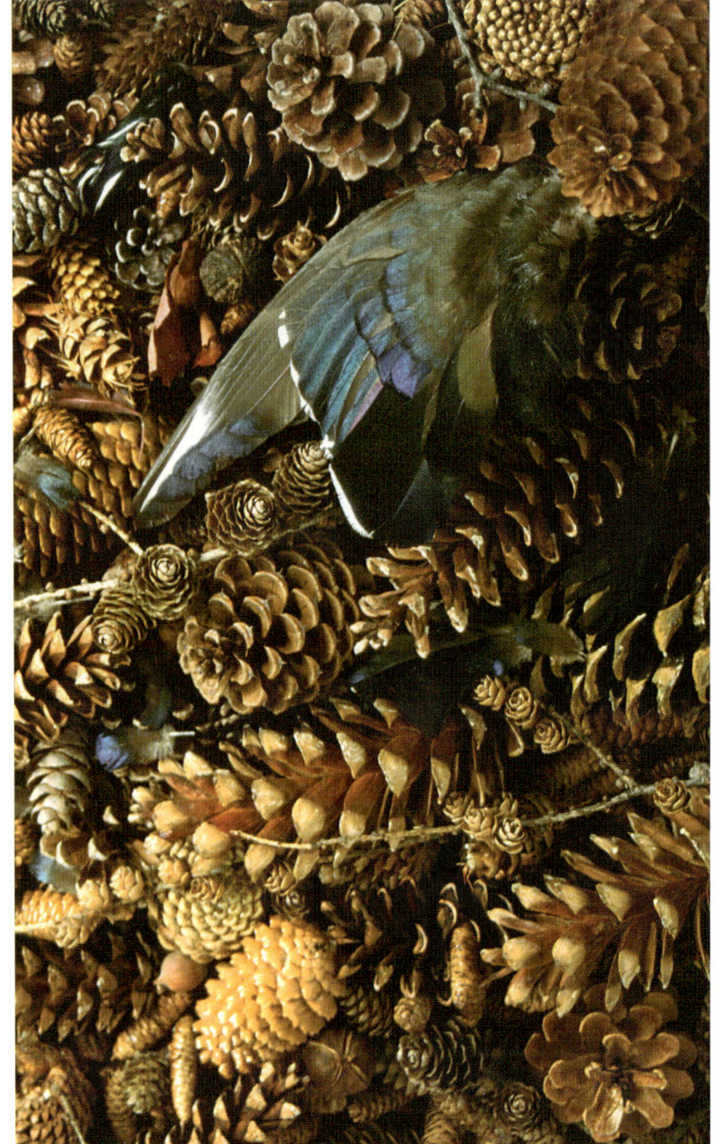

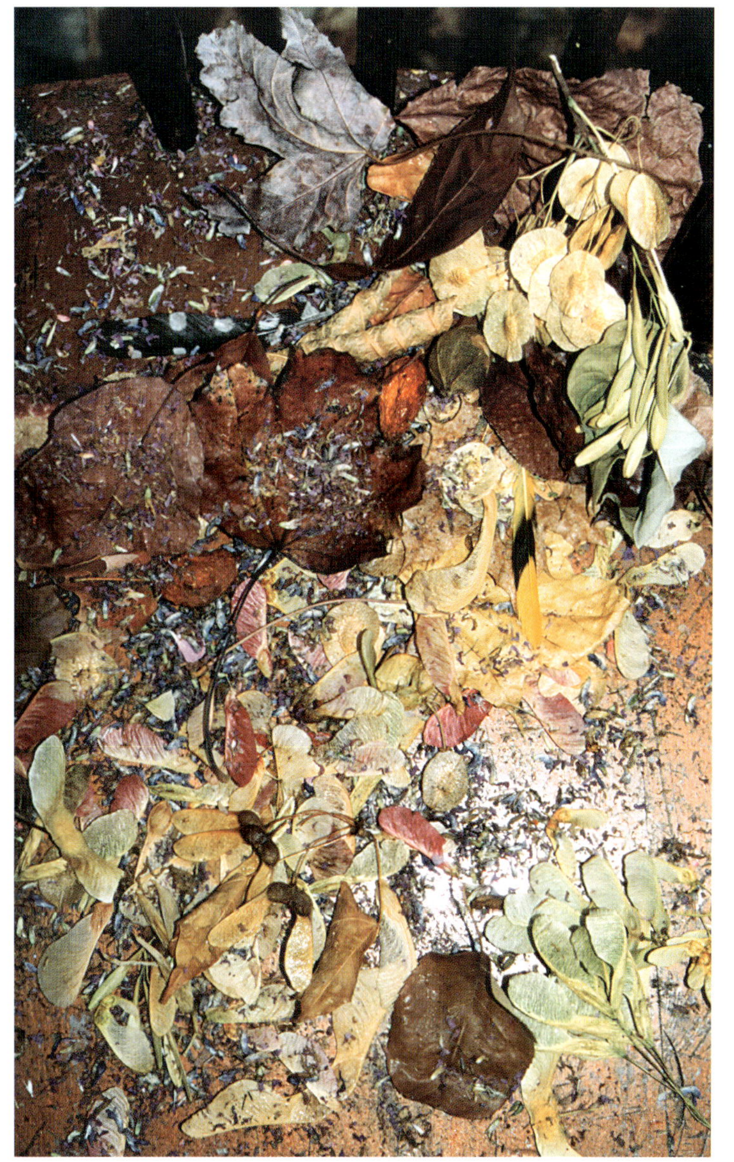

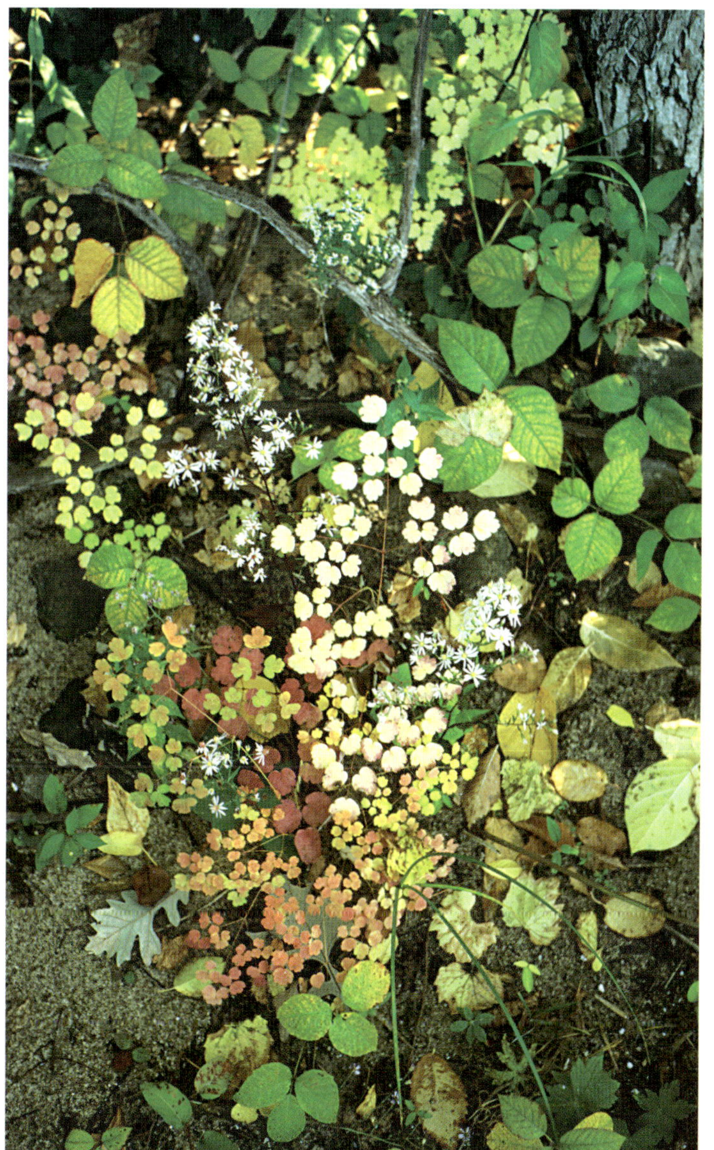

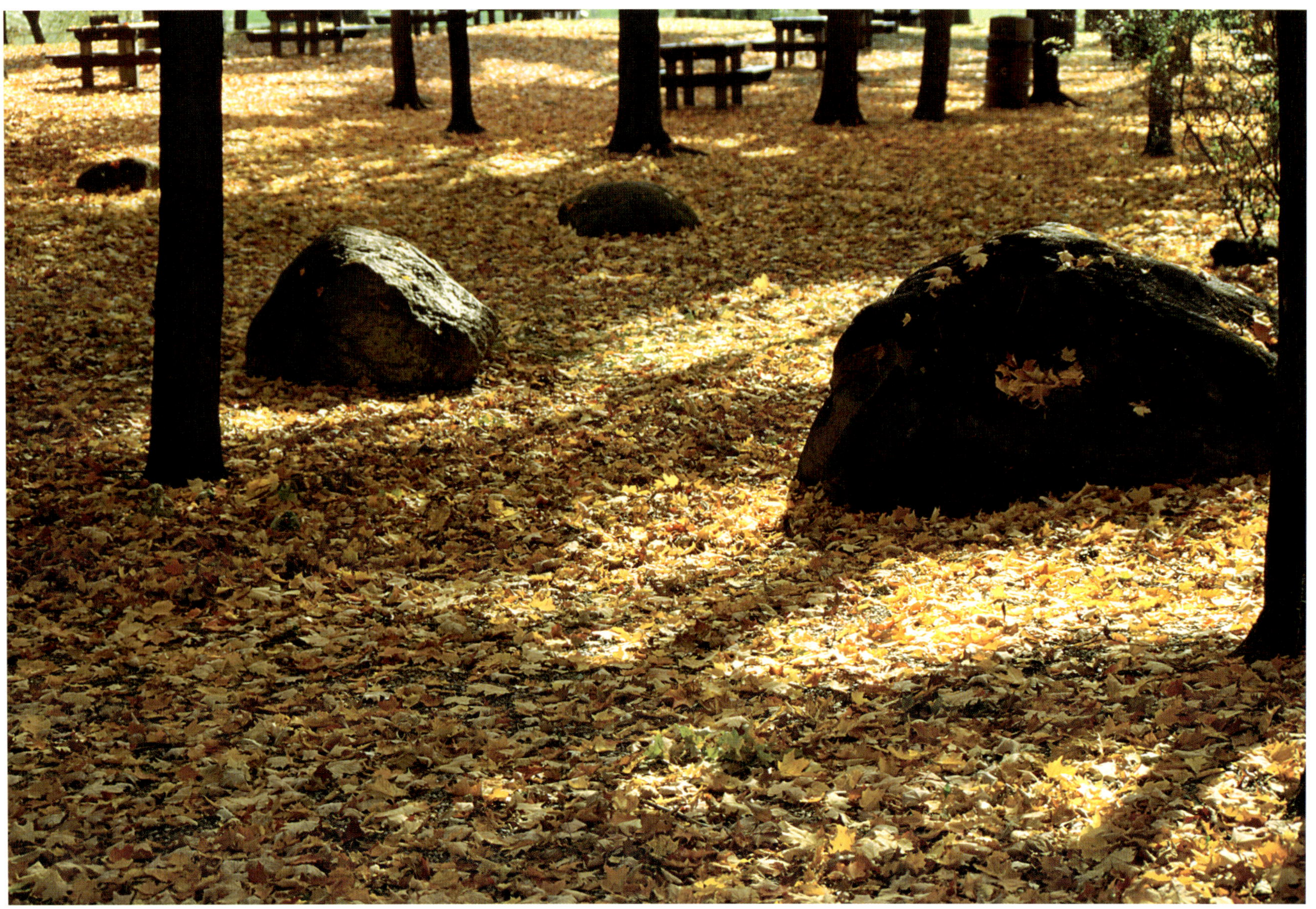

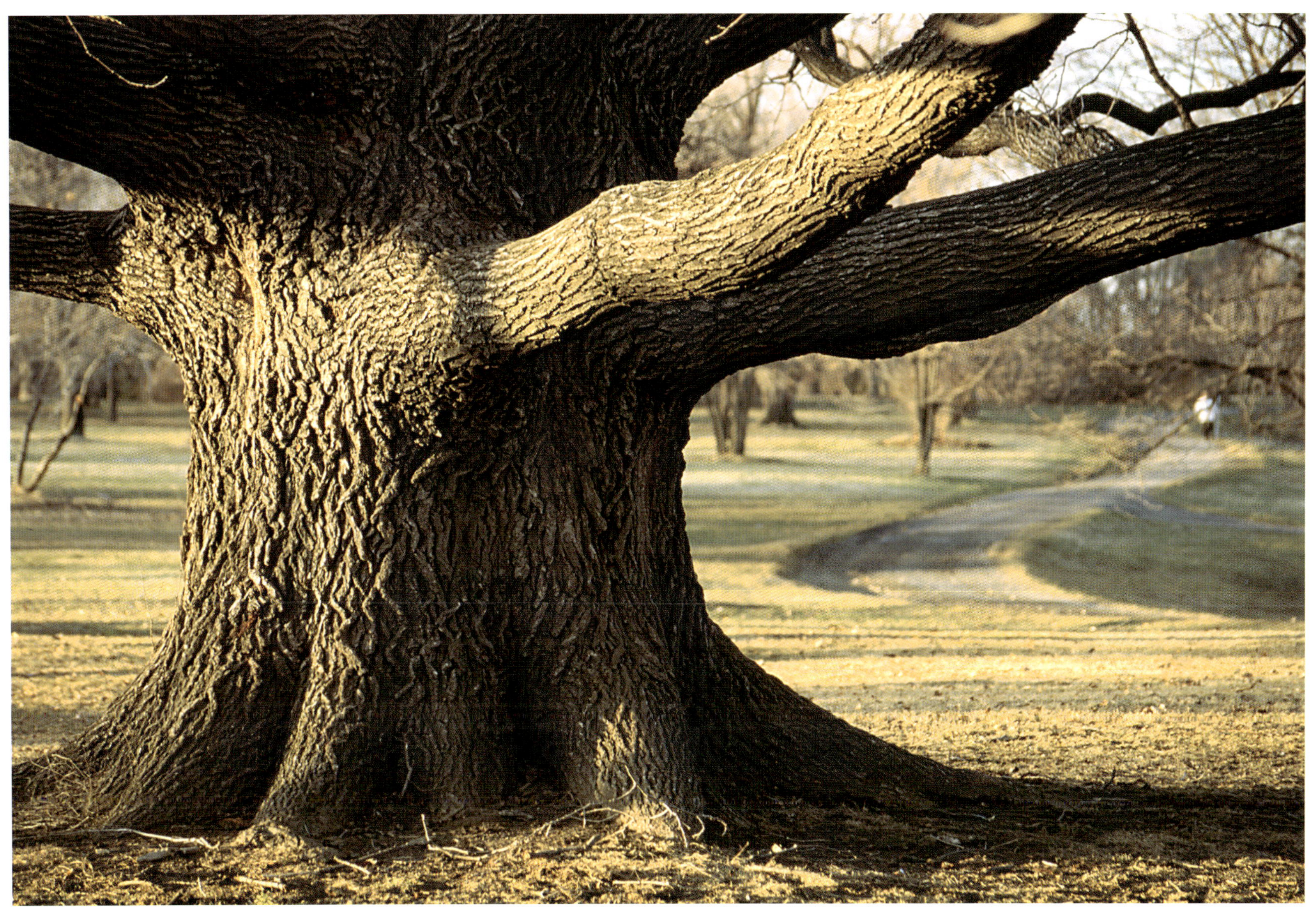

between the waxen corpse
and massed mums
someone sobs

calling
the geese leave
sadness

cloudy afternoon
a white chrysanthemum
just one

after the burial
only rain & bare oaks
distancing in rearview

through the mist
pale spires of spruce
a train whistle sounds

stiffening
on frost-curled leaves
a fawn's corpse

bitter words
in the dark — sleet
hitting our windshield

2 a.m.
& the donut shop
light goes out

under windswept skies
his white hair wild
the lockmaster shivers

down a wet street
the funeral cortège
of someone important

November
a cricket
in the rec-room wall

through the slot
with the pizza flier
a cold gust

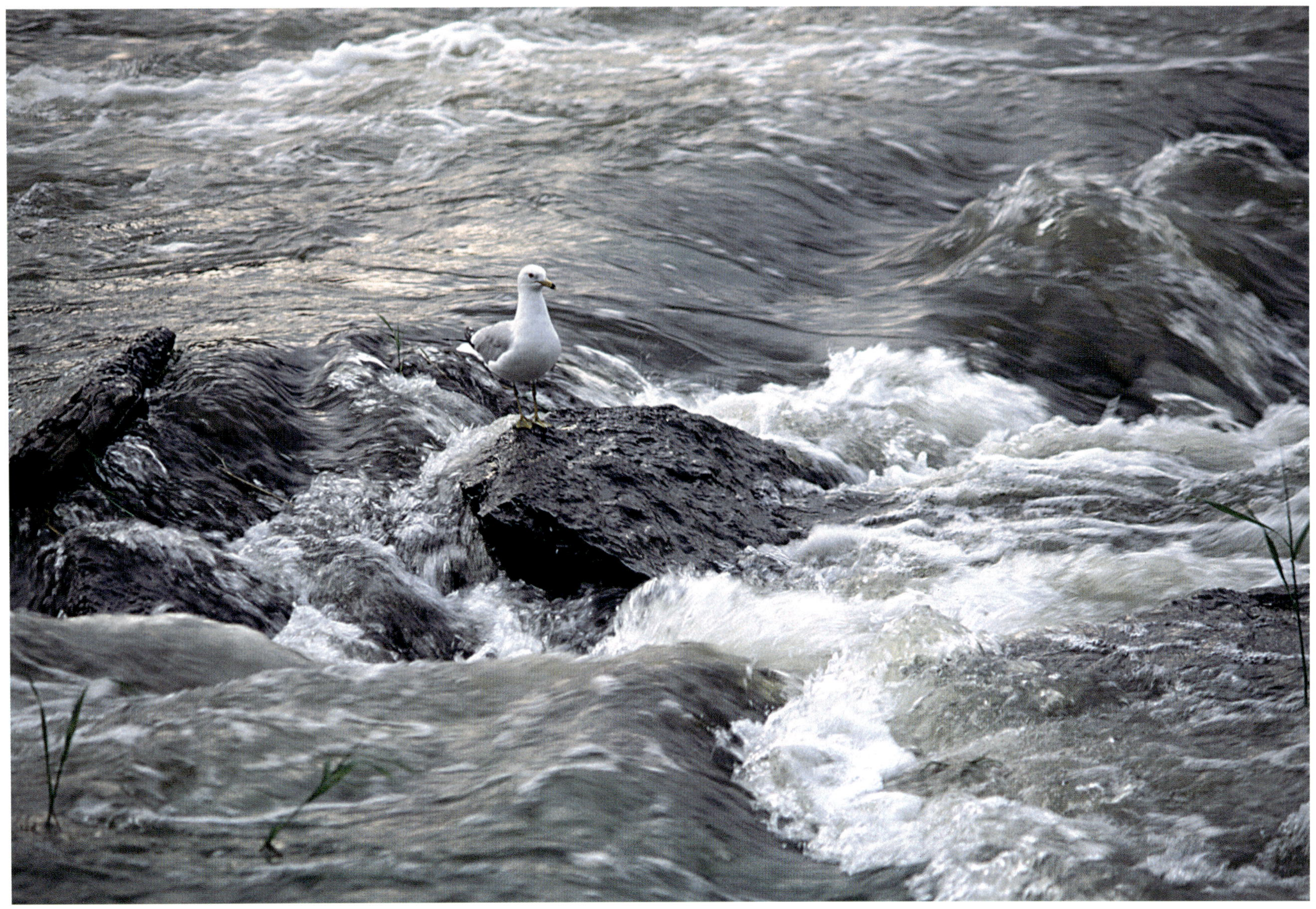

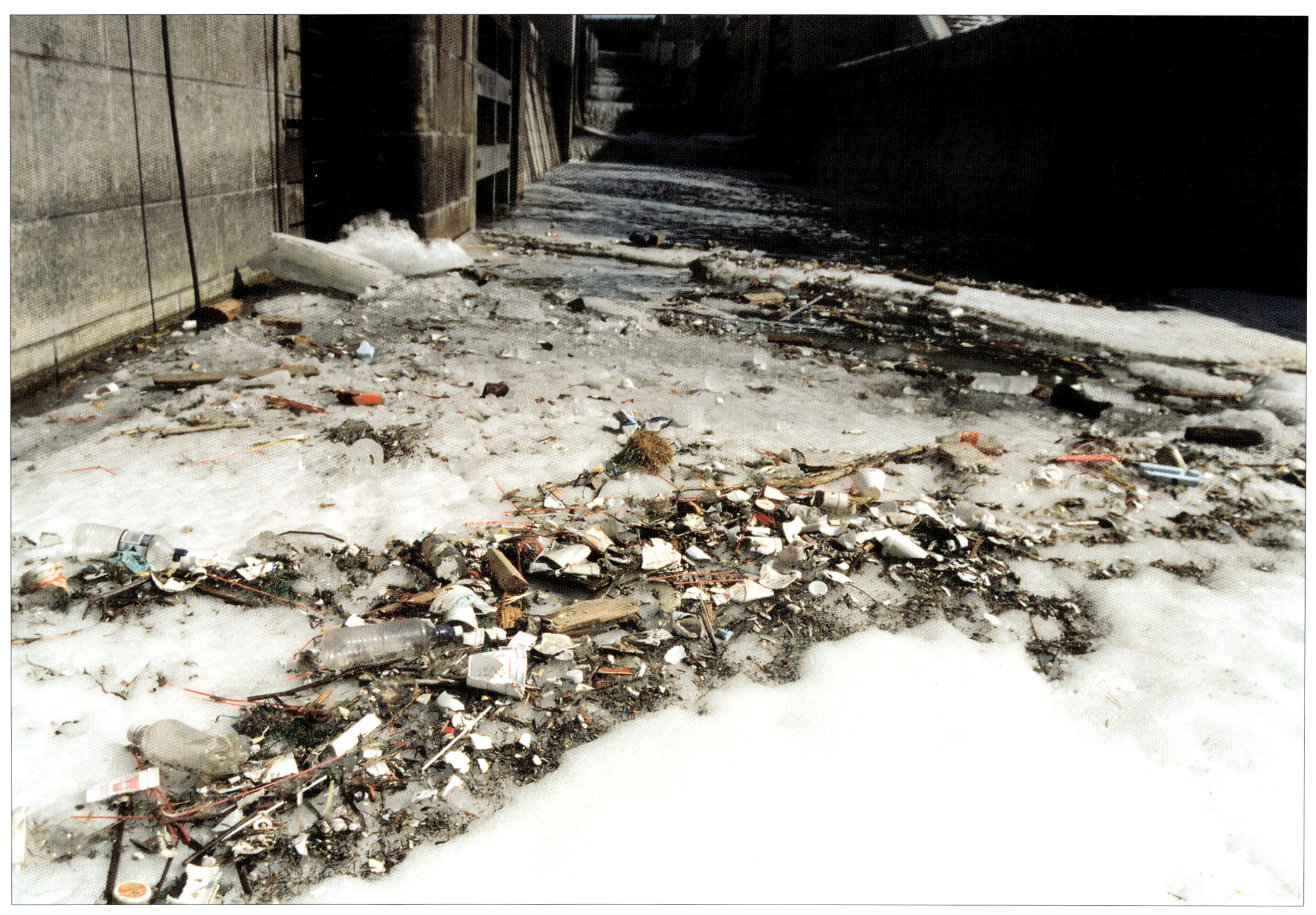

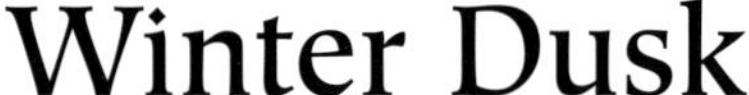
Winter Dusk

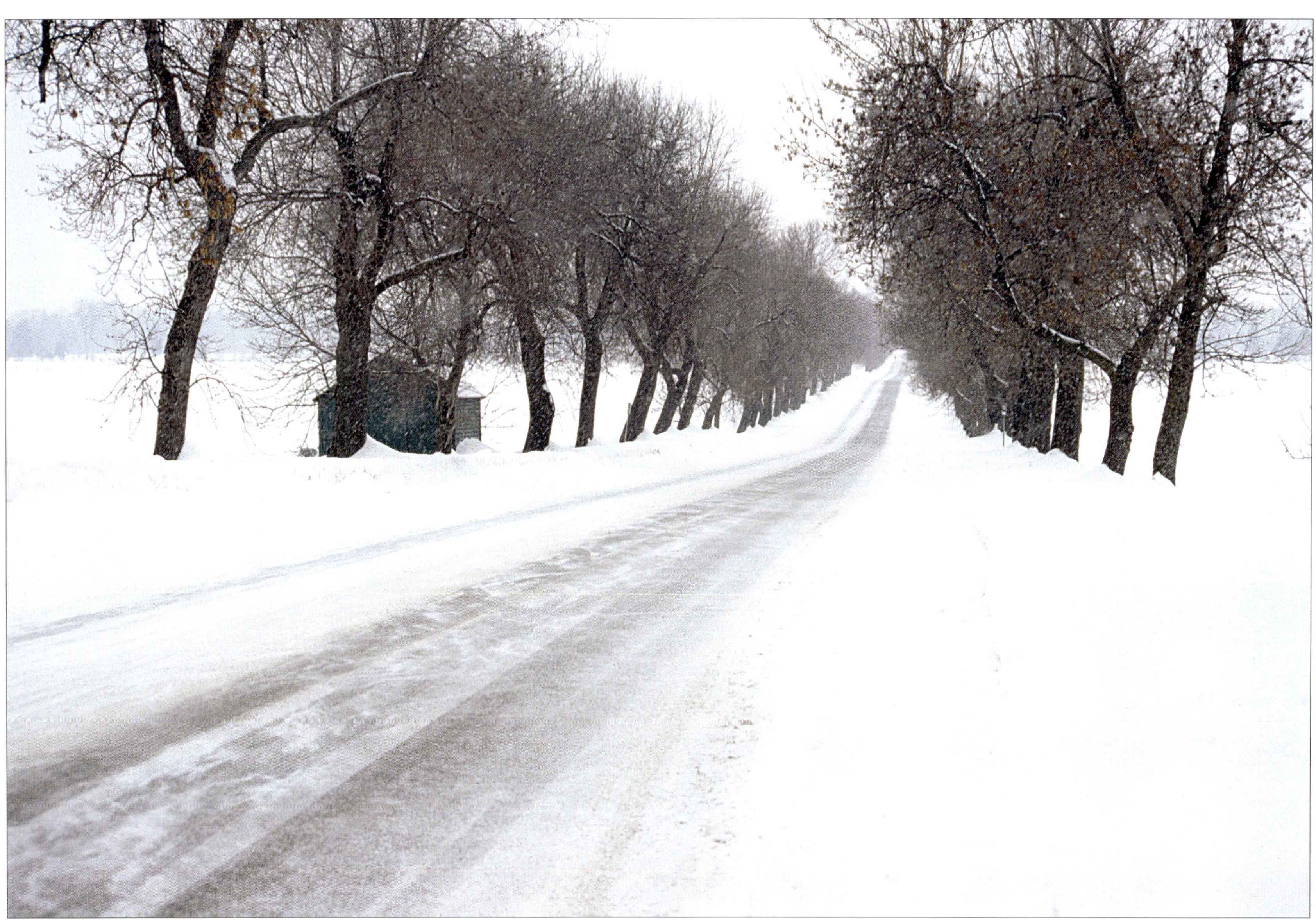

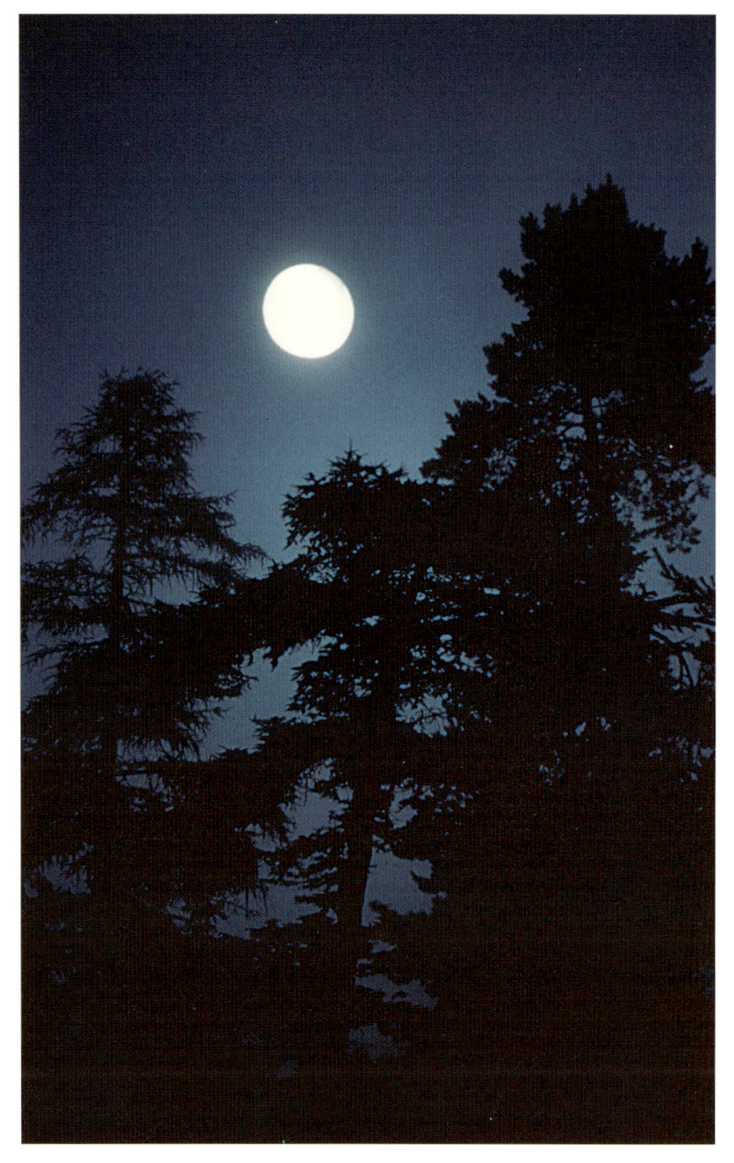

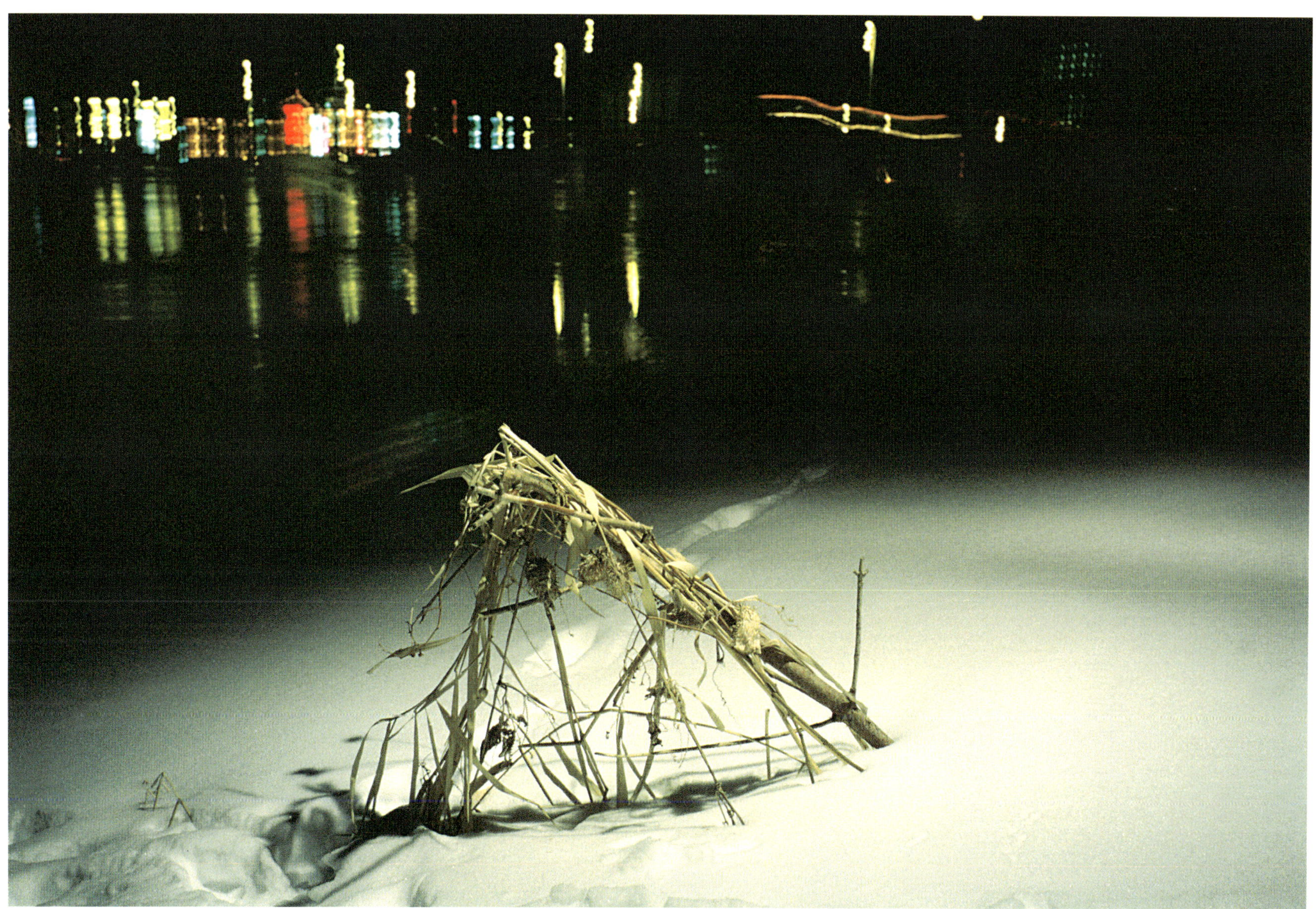

sun catching
the aquarium — fish
swim around the room

a rabbit
nips into its hole
windless chill

awakened by cold
as dawn cracks
the black woods

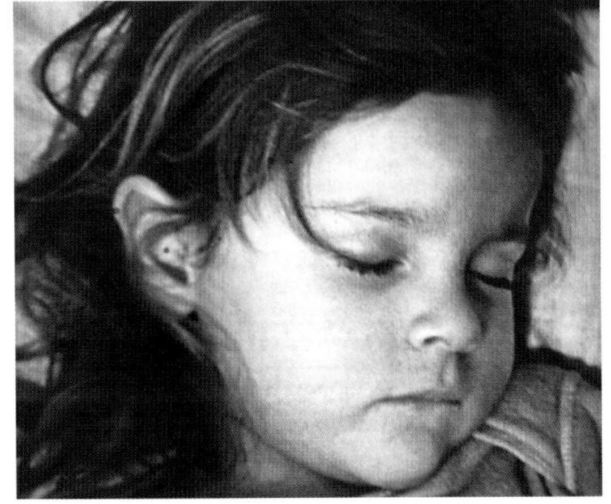

in the darkened office
moonlight fills
a styrene cup

splayed in the dust
among my books
that ragged moth

white smoke
streaming from factories upriver
the onset of winter

first snow
brightness in the kitchen
the chili bubbles

in hope of birds
on the sill by his computer
binoculars

in the windowless hall
of the luxury hotel
an infant's howl

thin light
only the shadows
of snowflakes

outside — a woodpecker
inside — my typewriter
pecking

I used to hate it
when my father wore
this battered hat

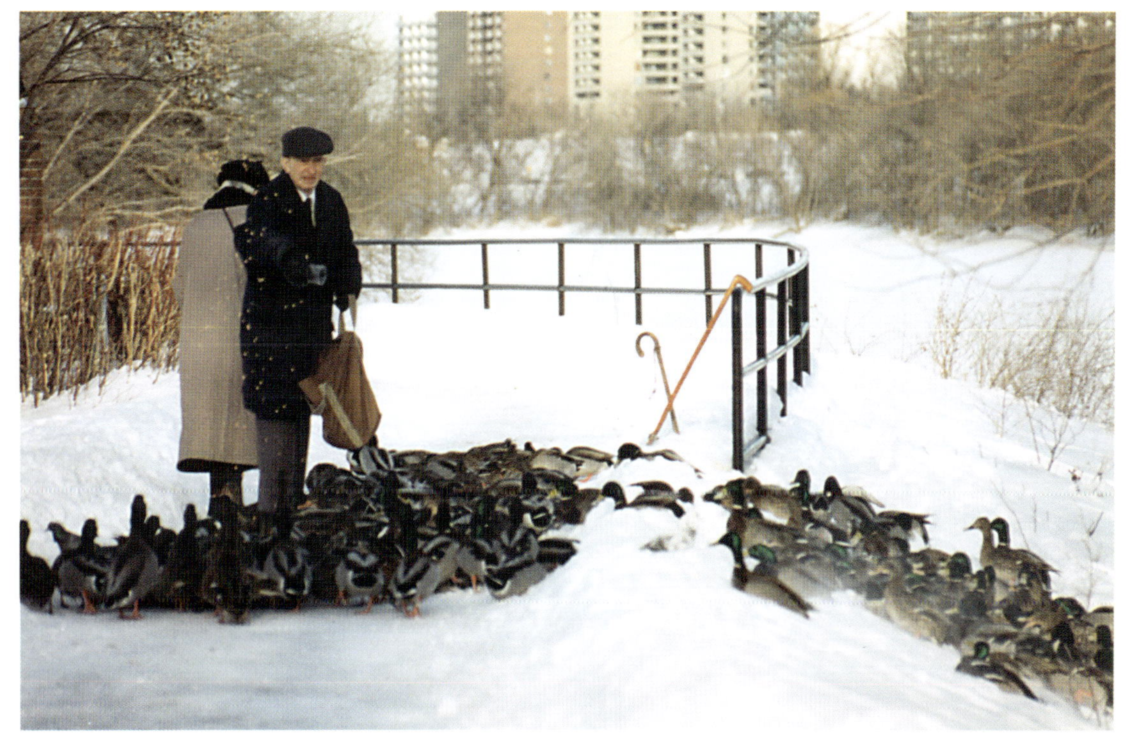

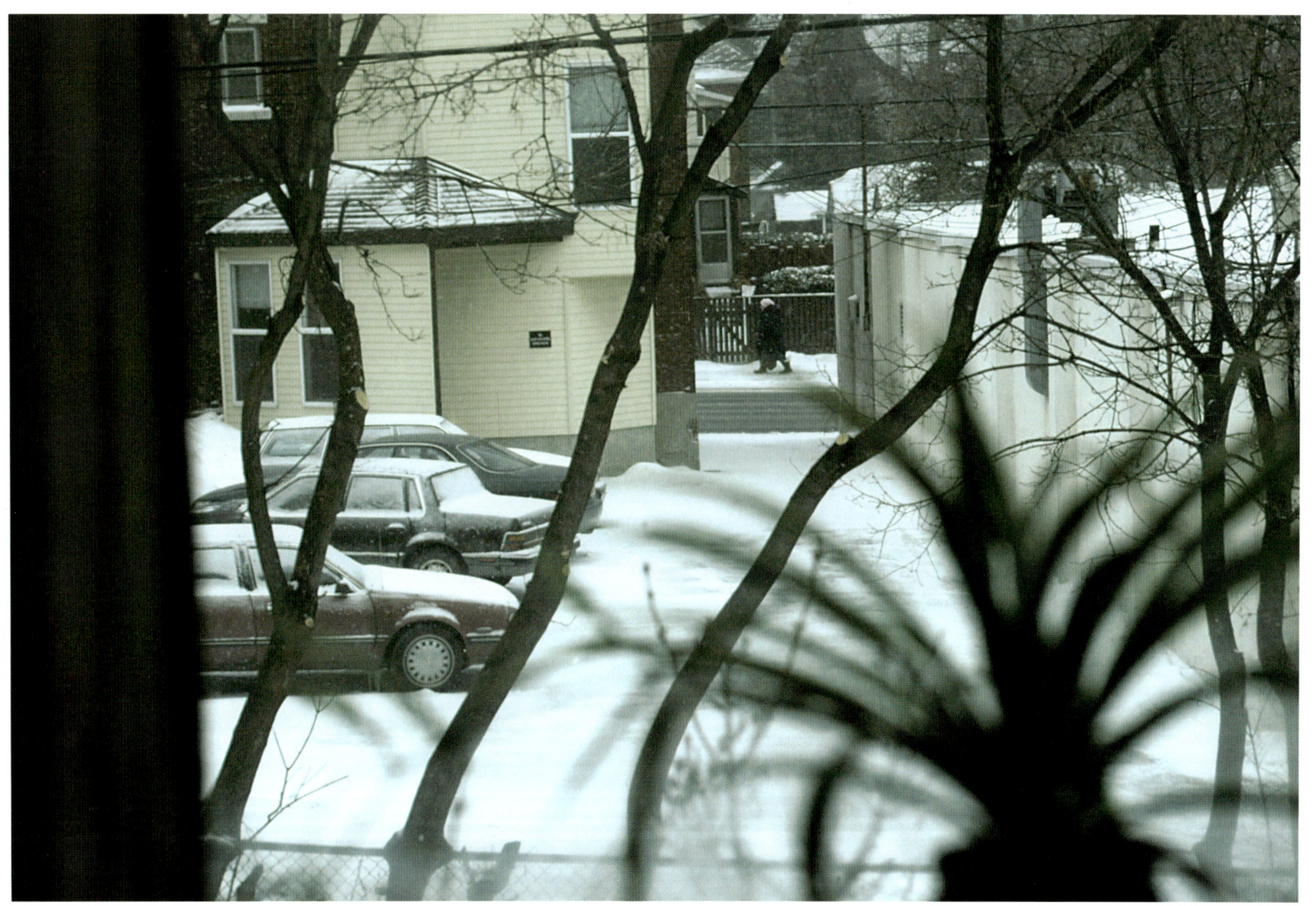

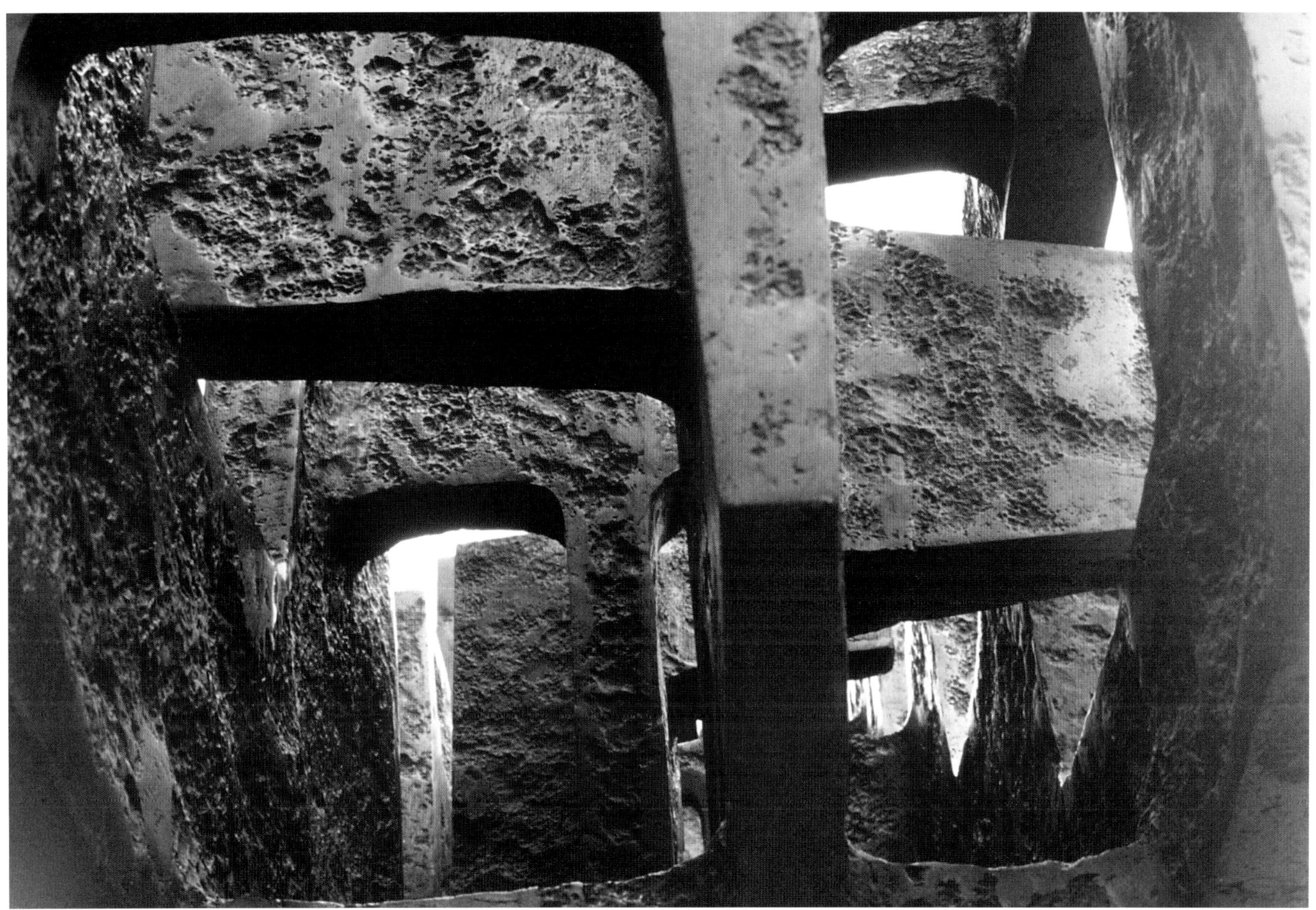

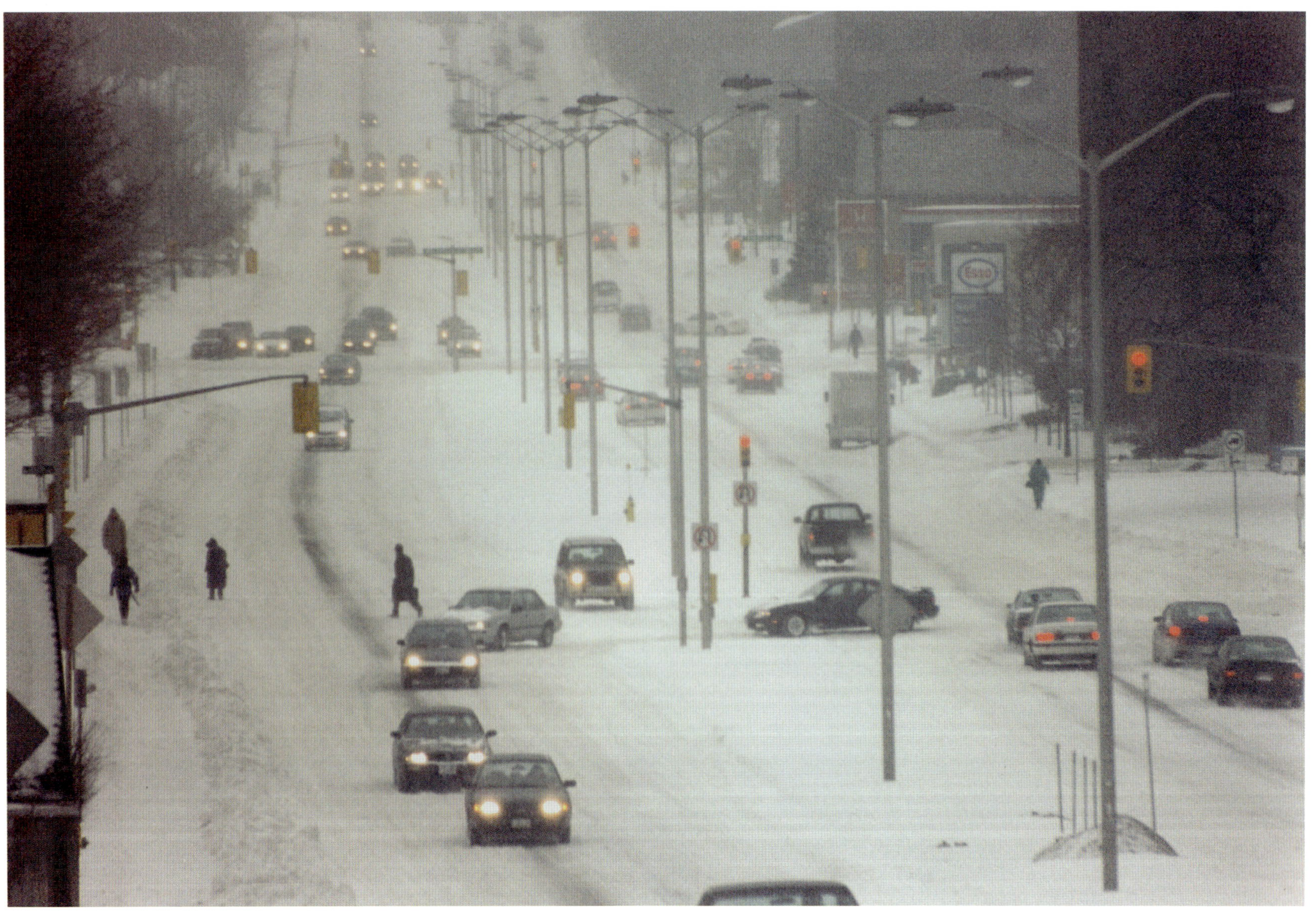
Esso

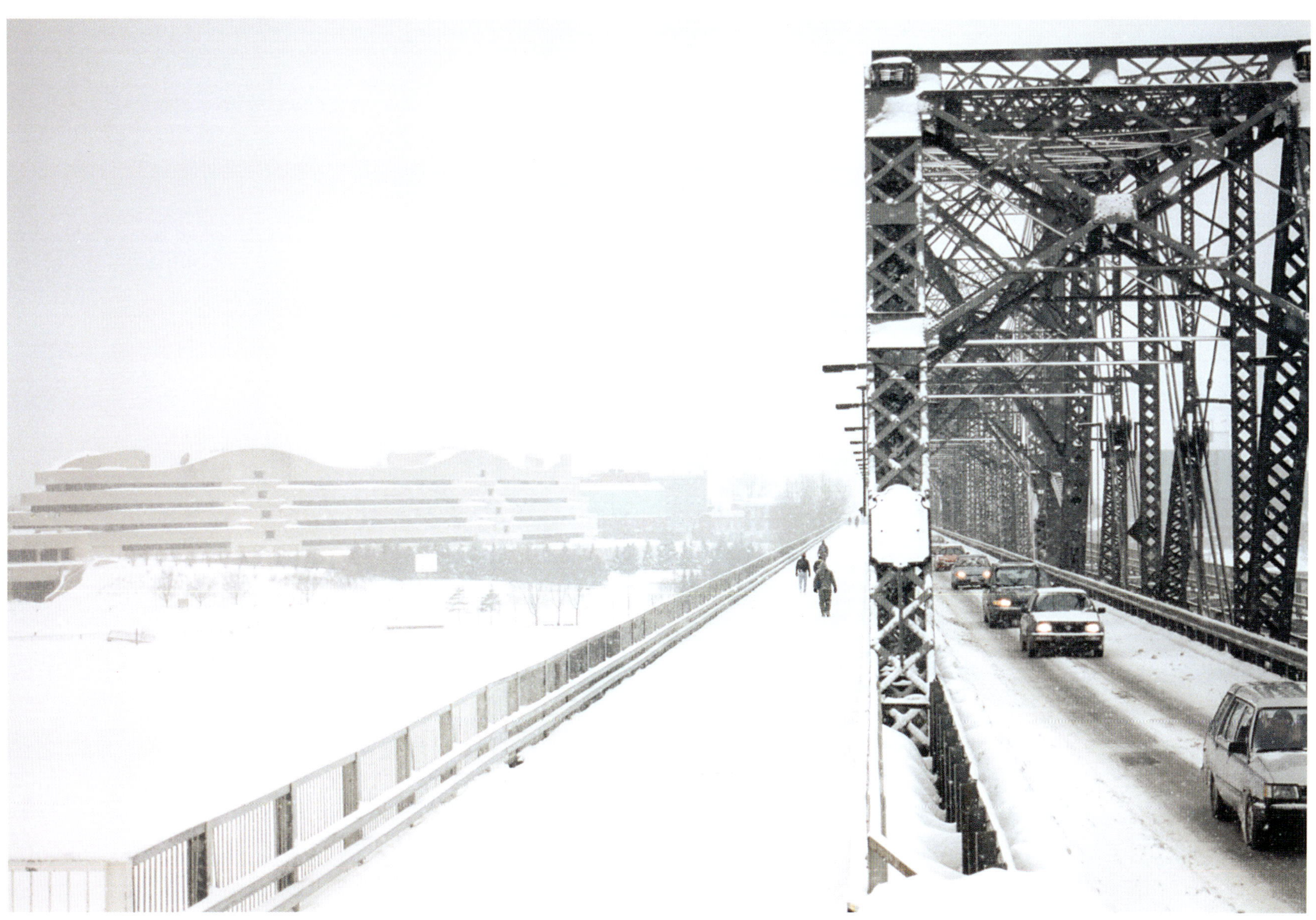

t.v. gunfire
the sleeping child's
eyelids flutter

past the cactus
in the window — shifting
flurries

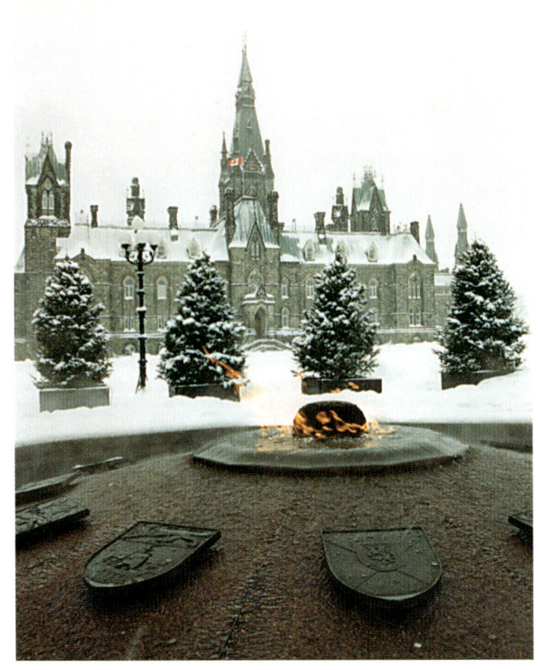

evening falls
I stand up
and walk around the room

applause
sweeping the poet
into darkness

moon shadows on snow
in a midnight park
elms creak

down the night ward
interrupting my pain
a nurse's flashbeam

pale begonias and
the highrise child's
disconsolate elbows

deep cold tonight
my neighbour's out shovelling
blue moonlight

outside the cancer clinic
a huddle of nurses
smoking

mid-winter
in a shoebox of seashells
a few grains of sand

snowbound
with mice
that scratch in the walls

the old clock
ticking as my husband
turns a page

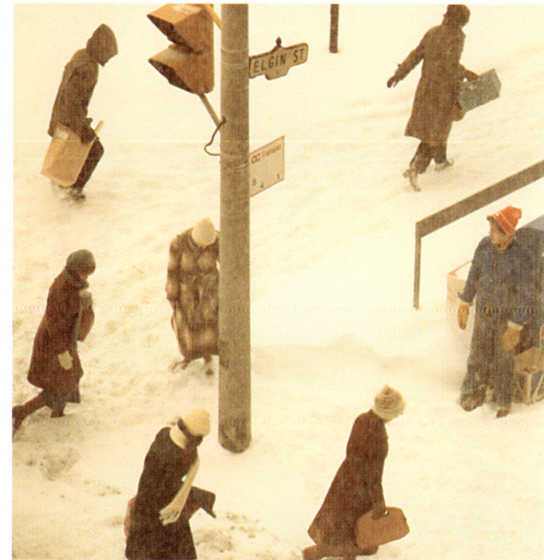

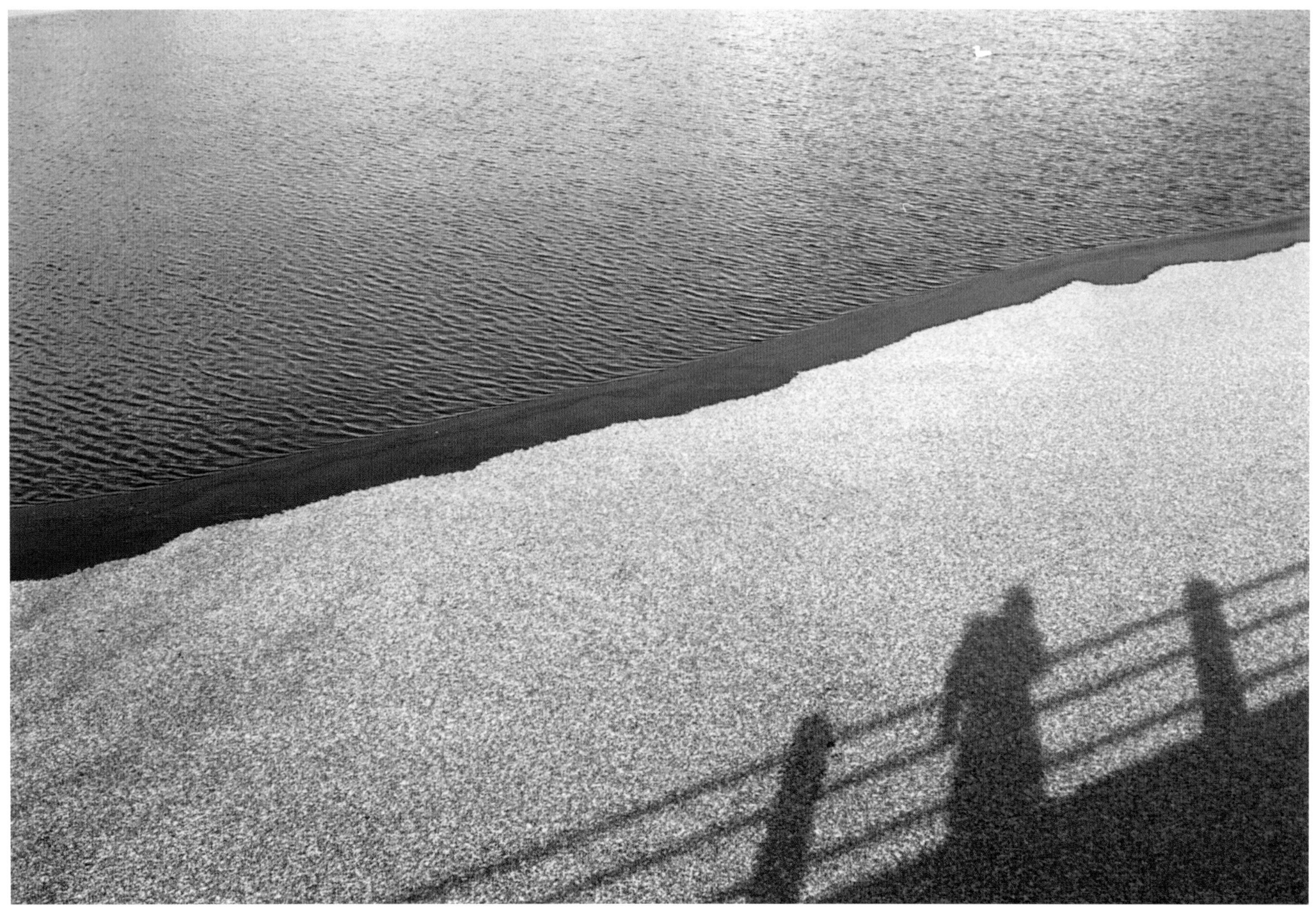

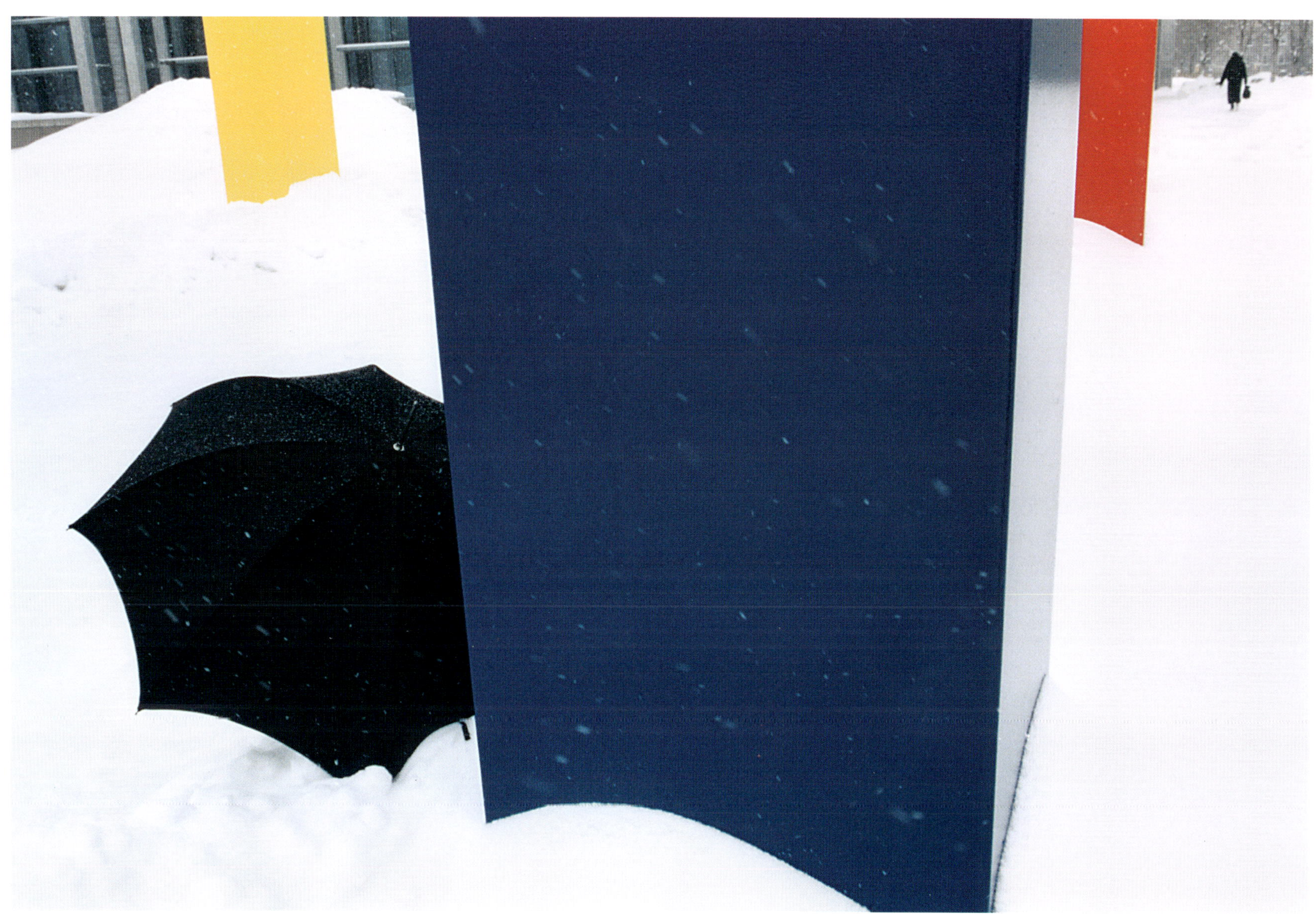

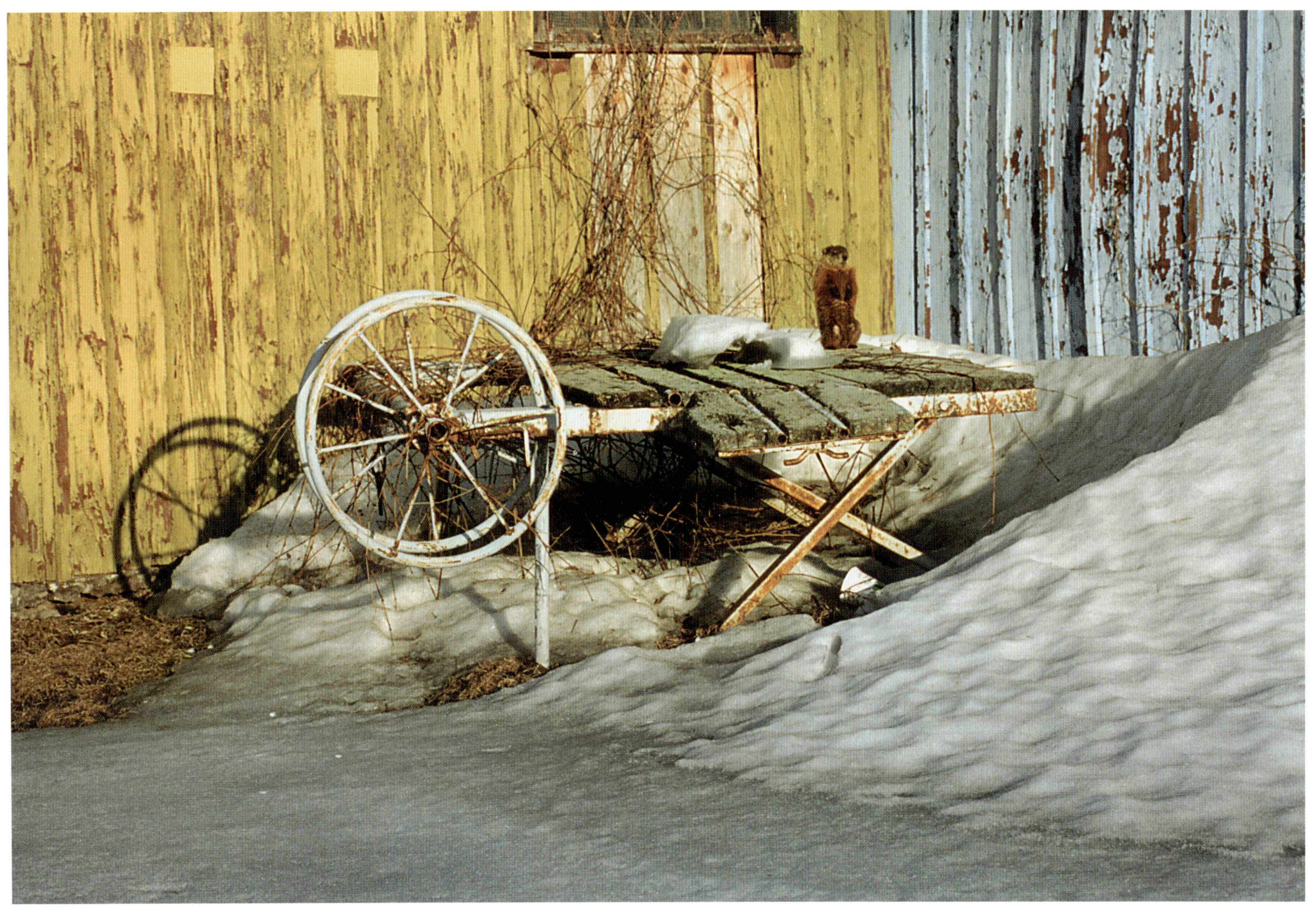

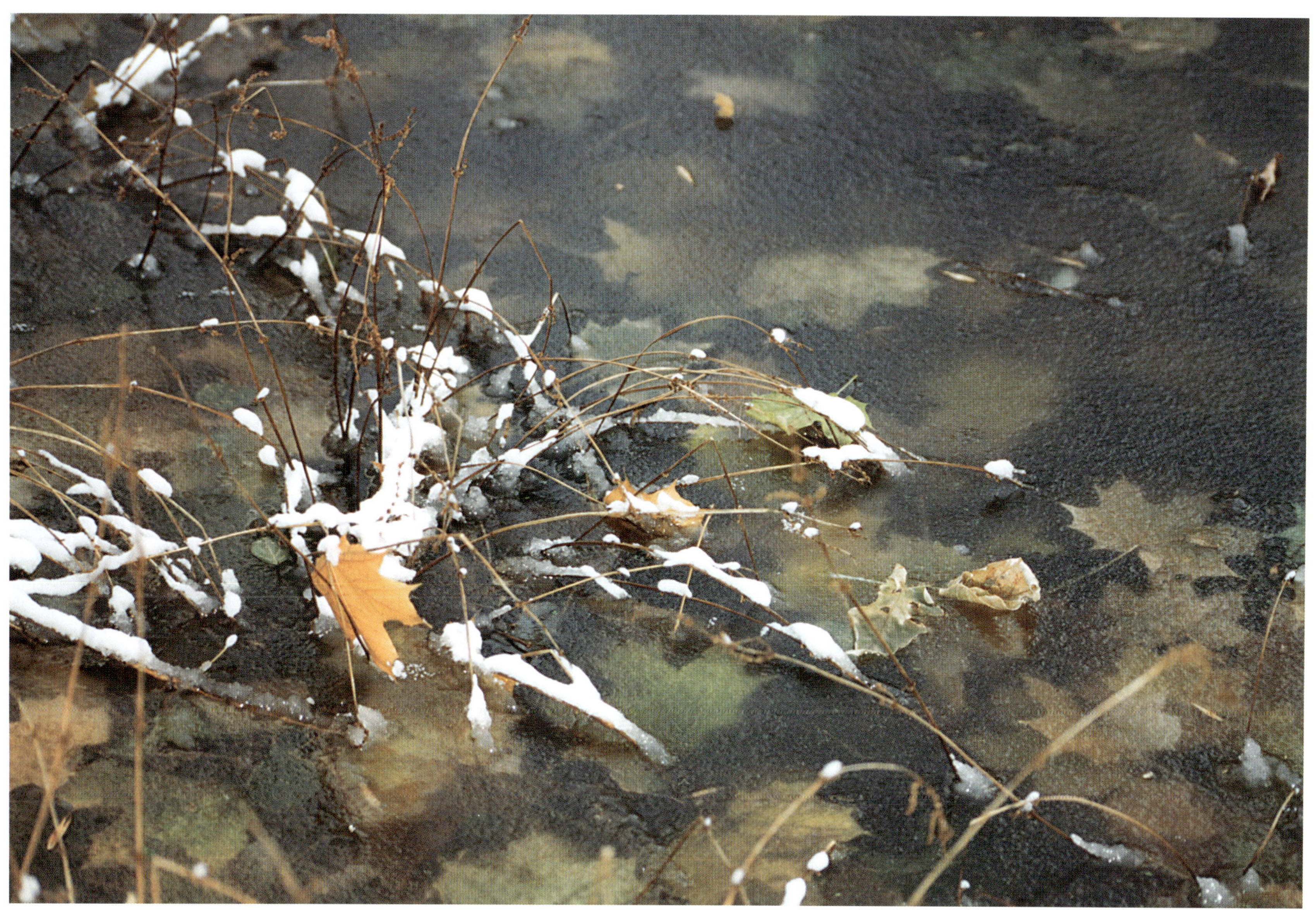

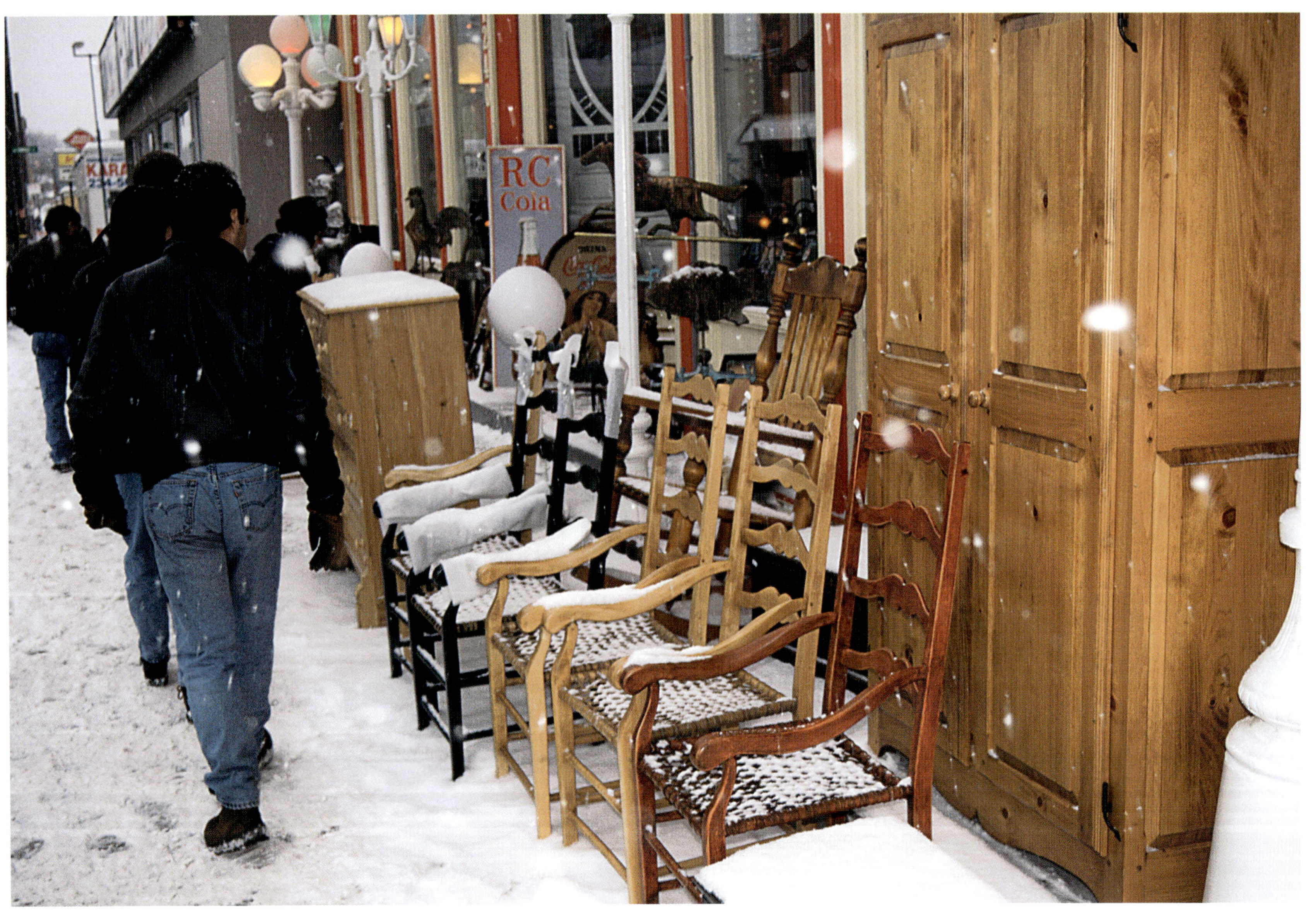
RC
Cola

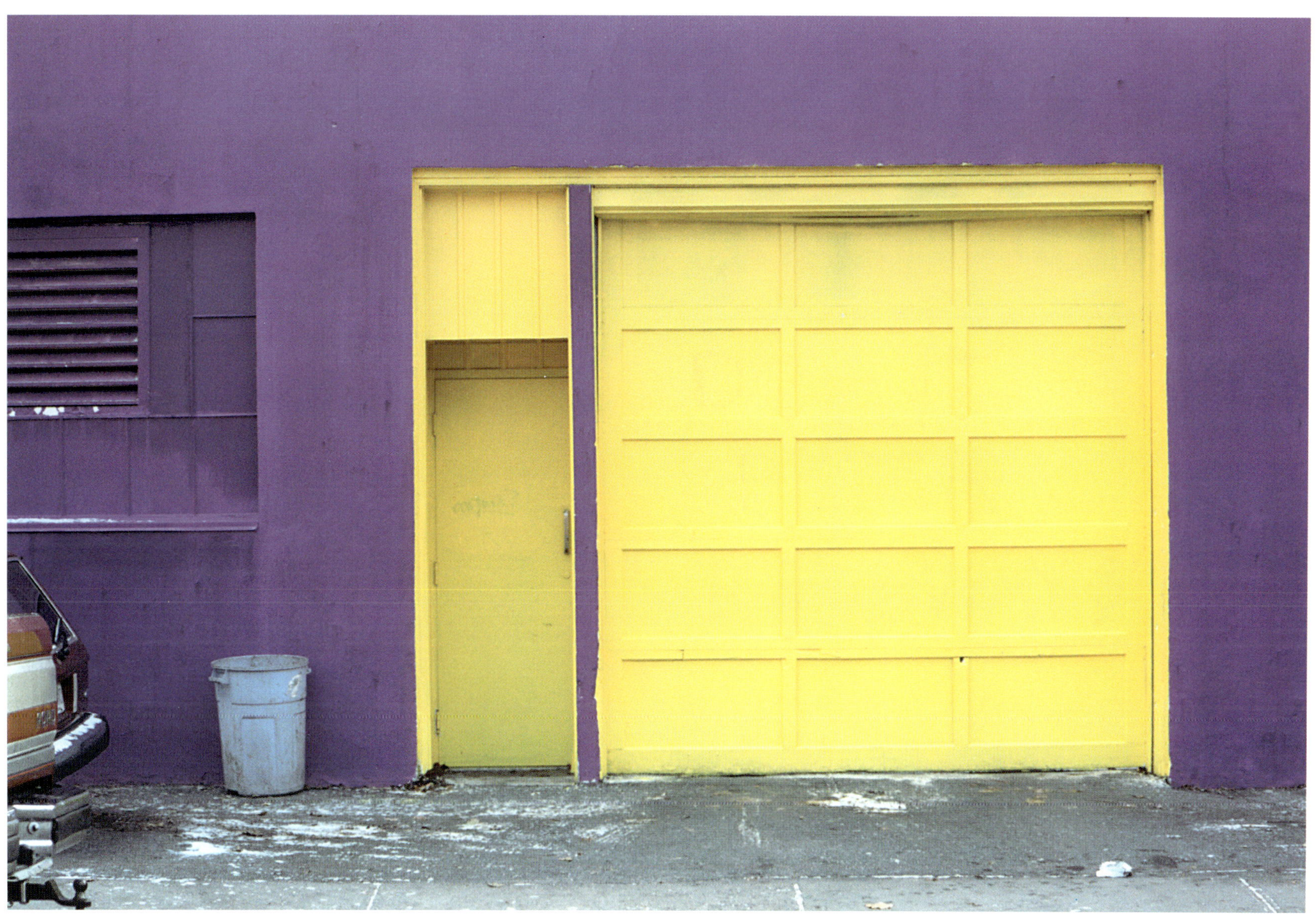

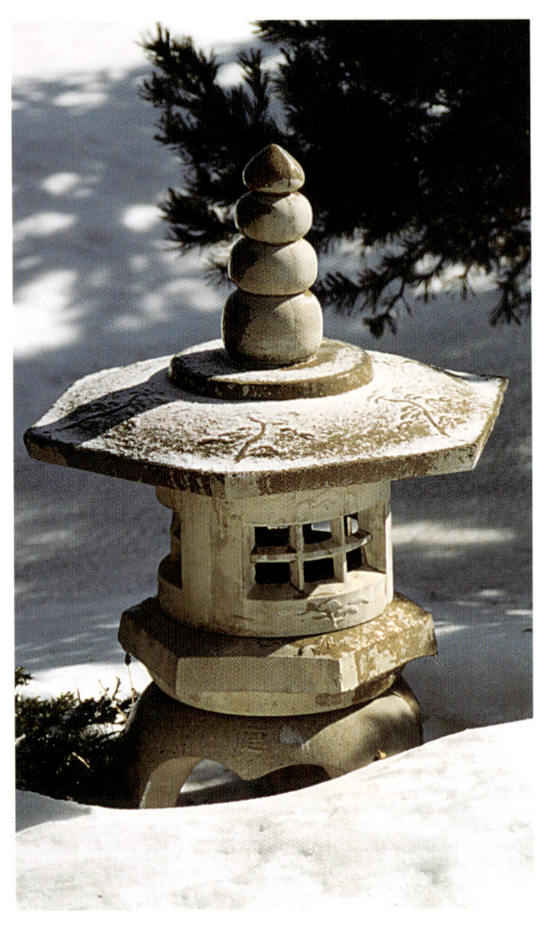

with the tip of her cane
touching fresh snow
New Year's morning

for the panhandler too
the first workday
of another year

through freezing rain
beating down on the stripmall
a gull

a dog's baying
echoes across the backhills
winter dusk

stopped cold in housewares
ambushed
by emptiness

past midnight
the phone rings — again
I don't answer

the drunker I get
the clearer it shines
that moon

in elms
above the snowball fight
crows shout

in the yellow lamp glow
long-haired Agi
reading fairy tales

first mauve of dawn
& the donut shop
light comes on

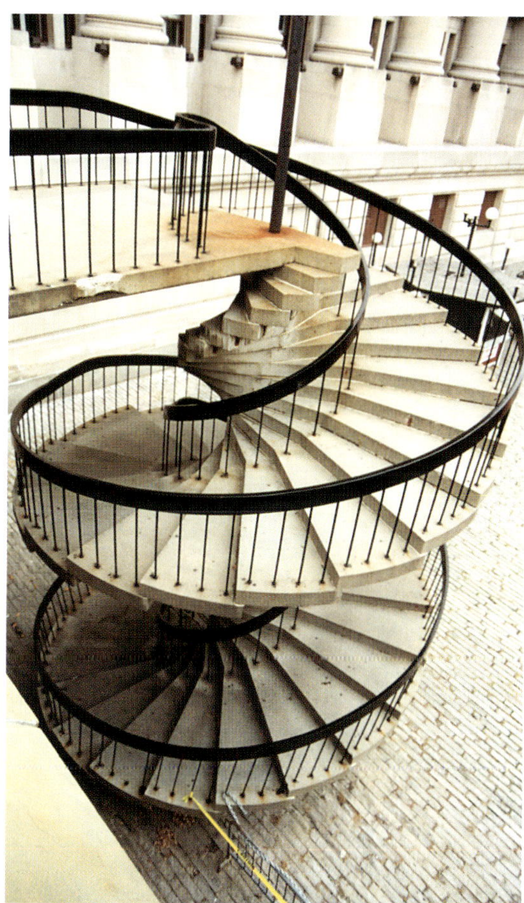

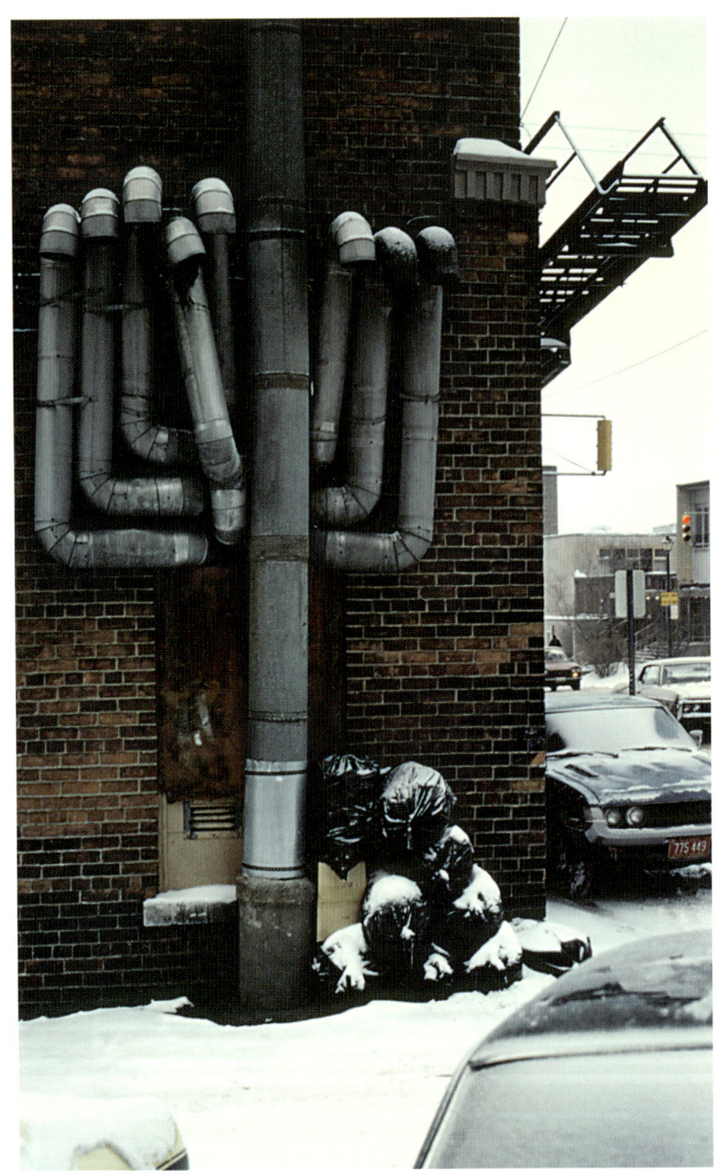

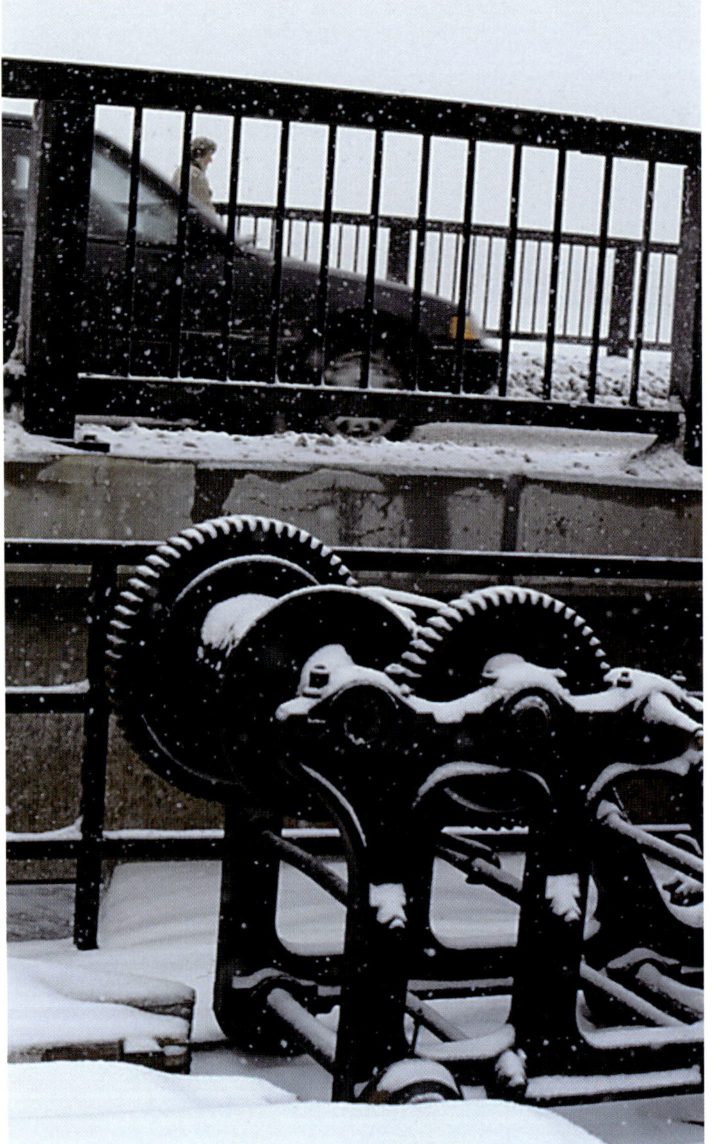

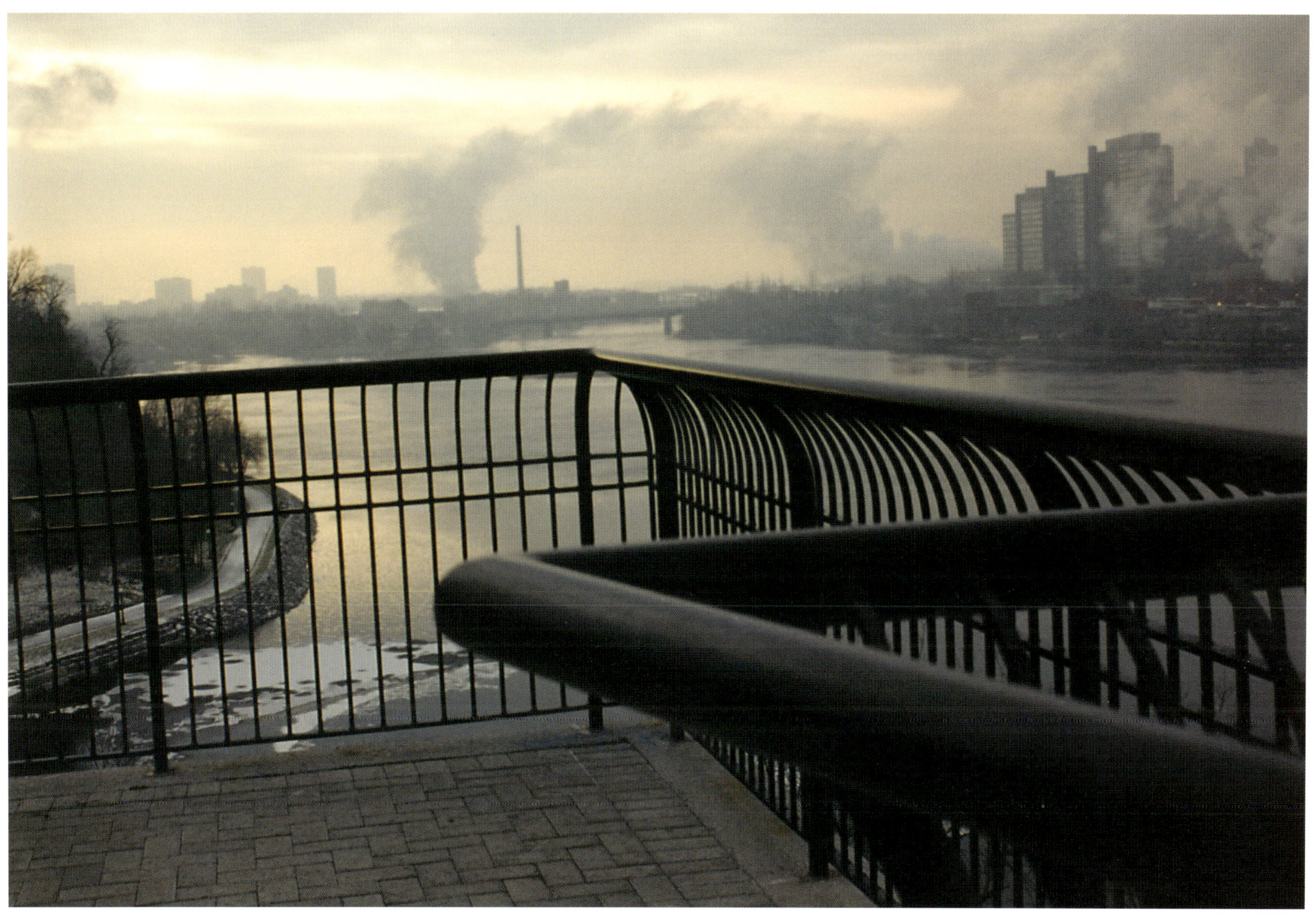

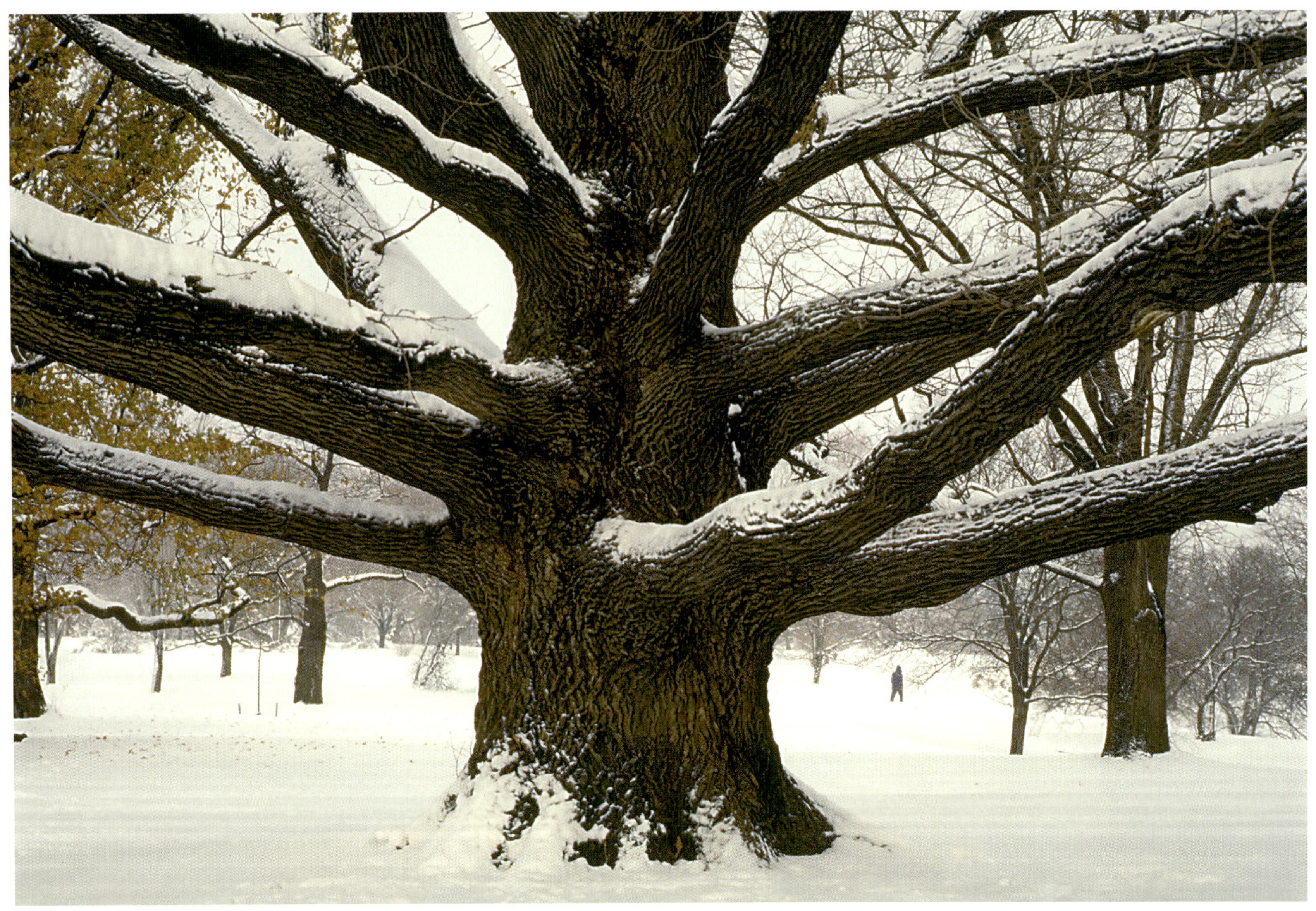

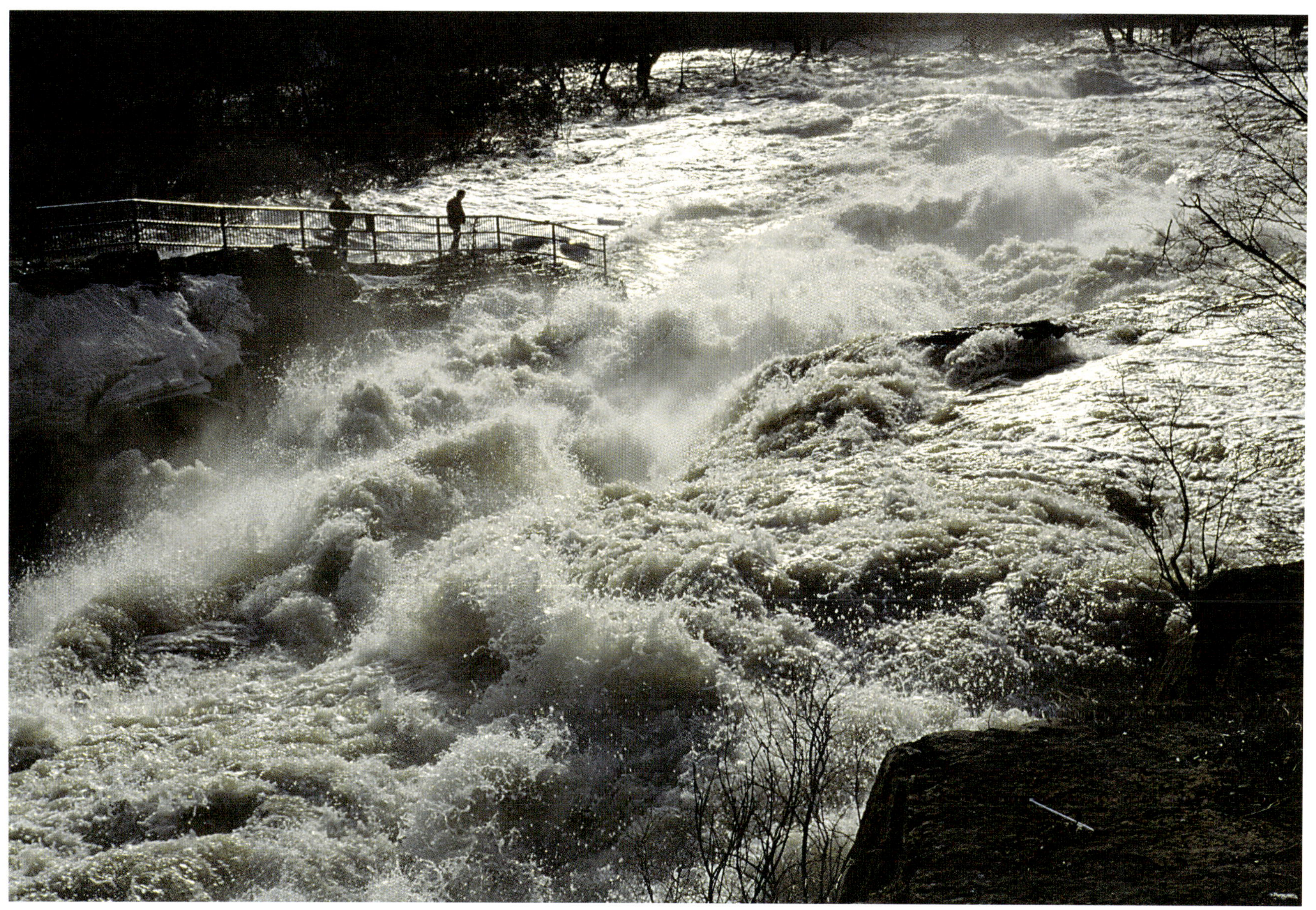

Loam

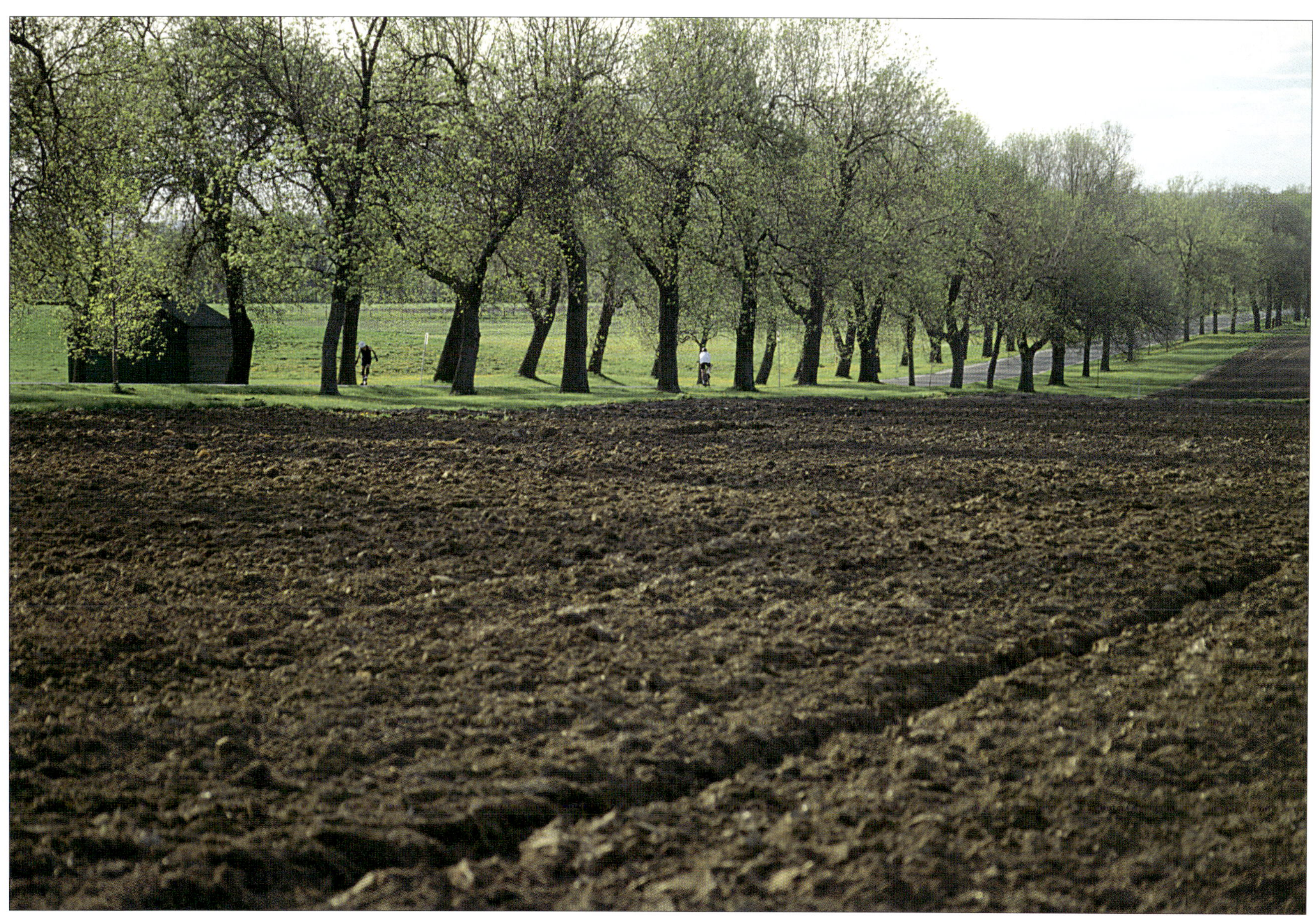

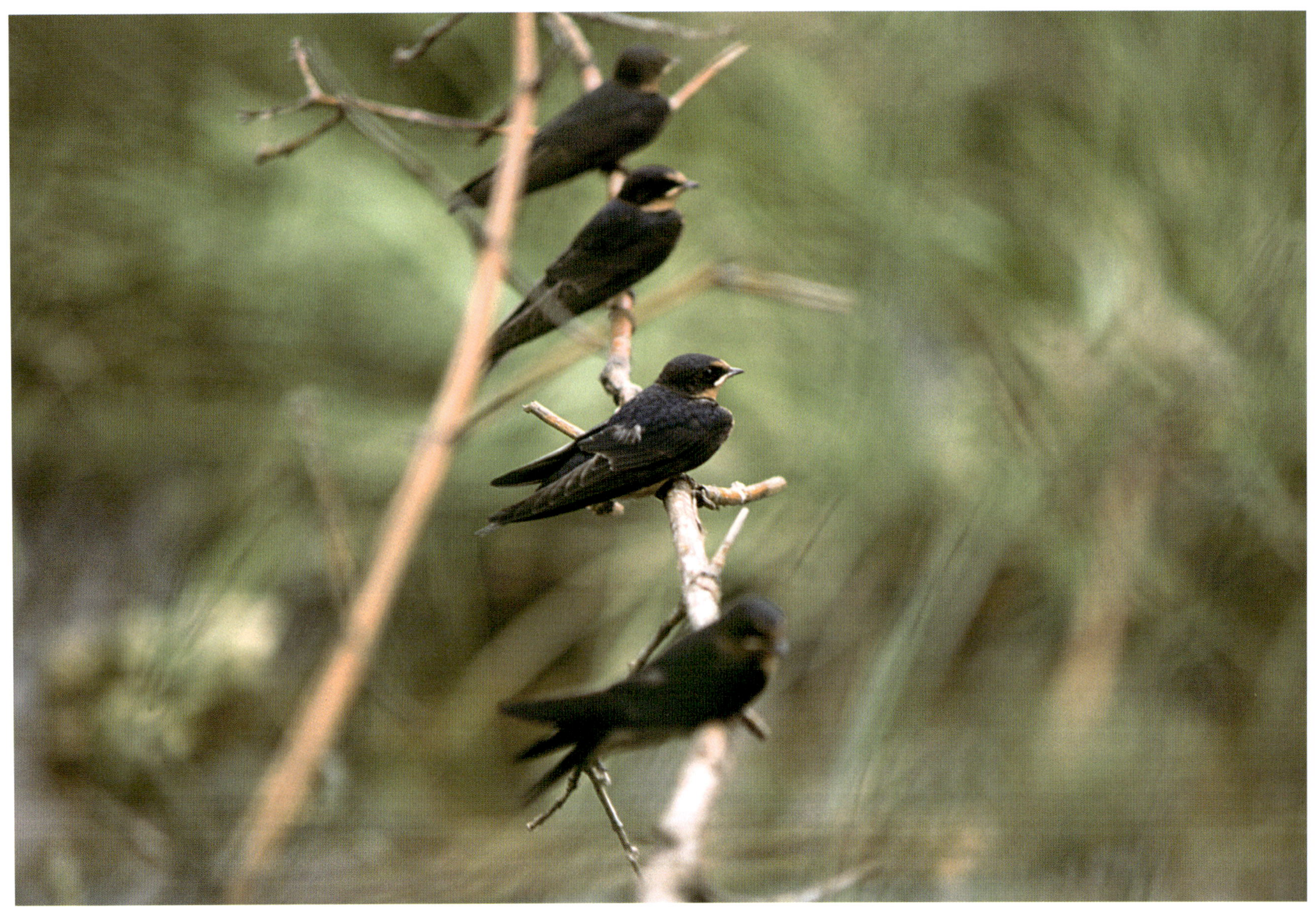

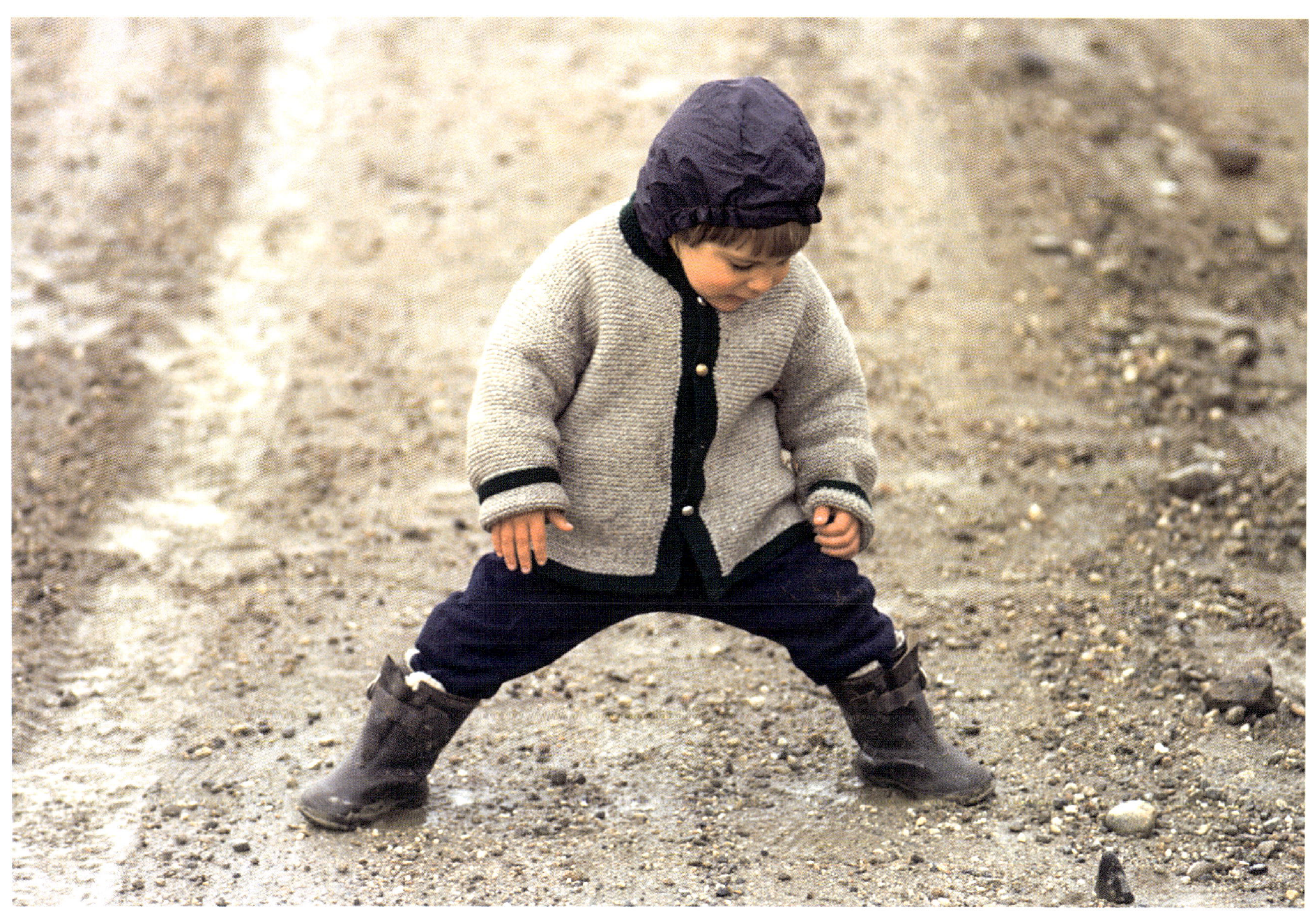

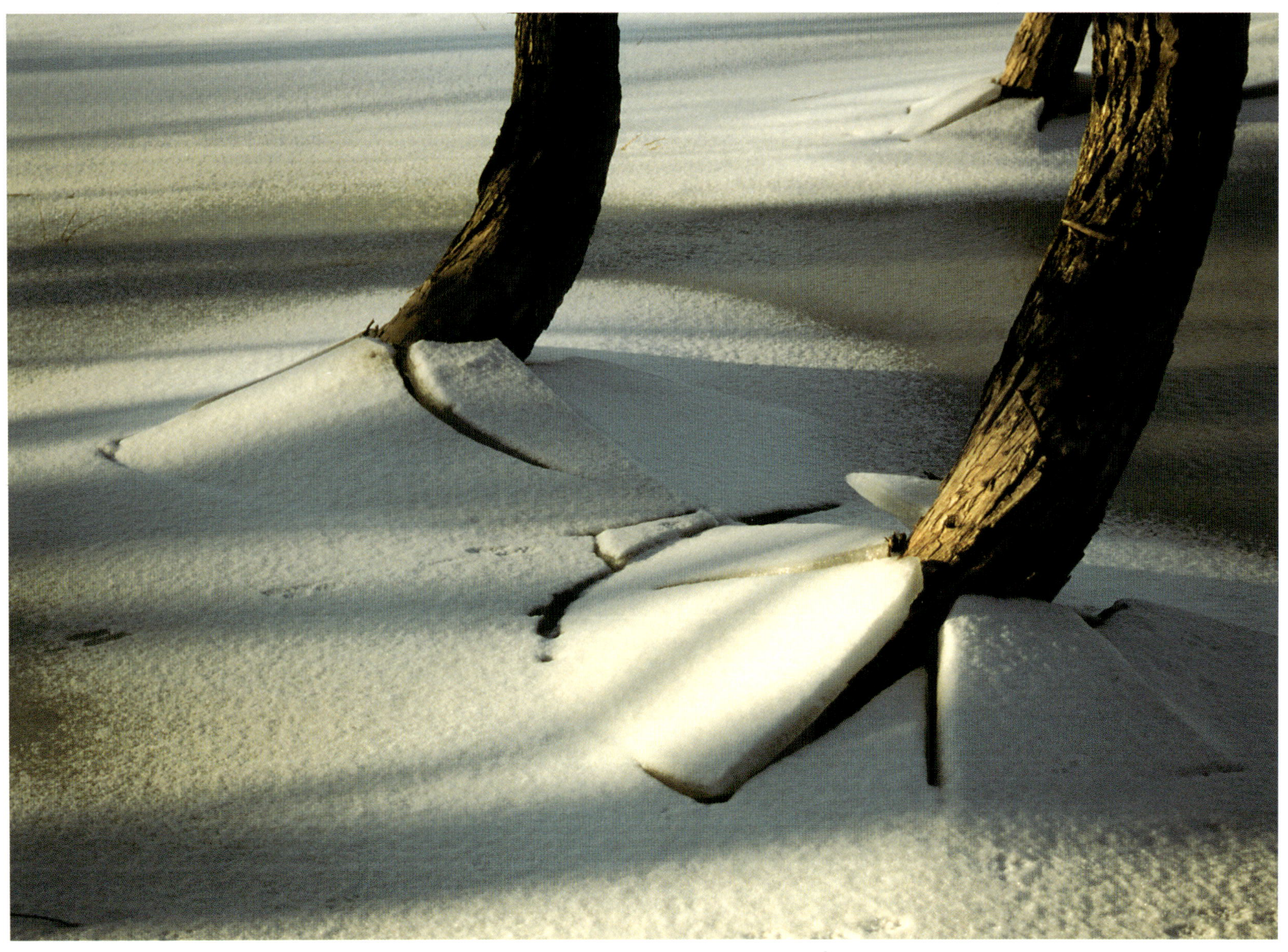

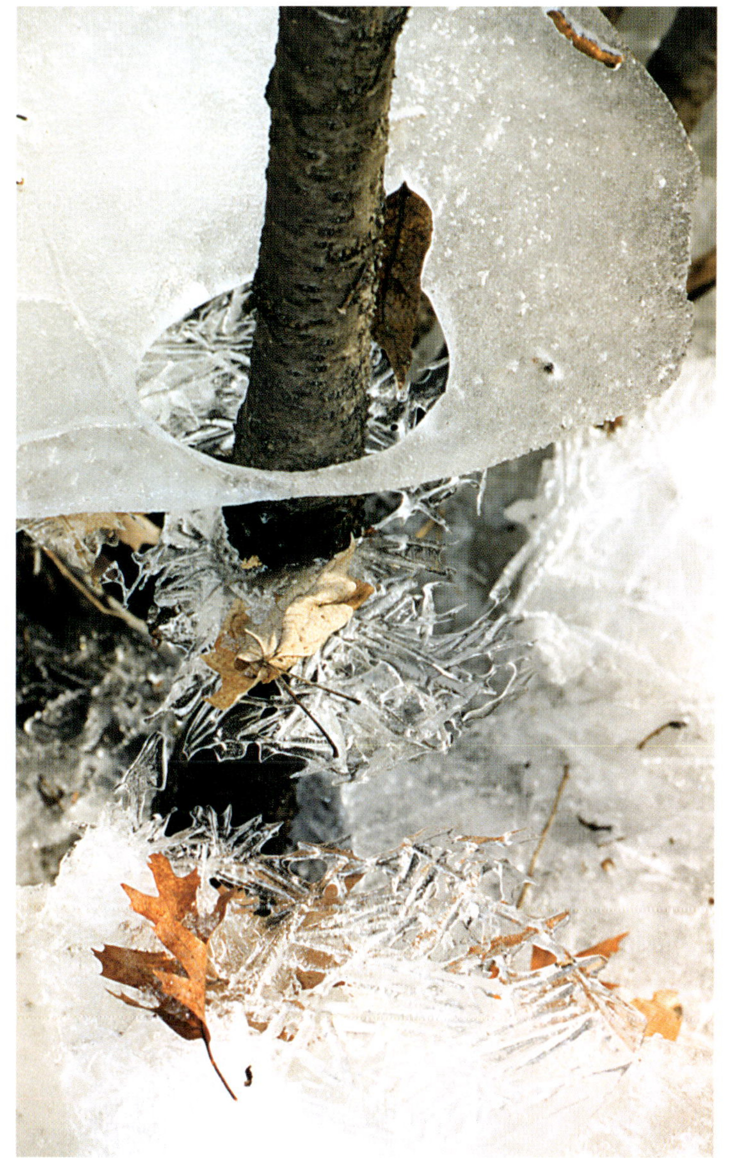

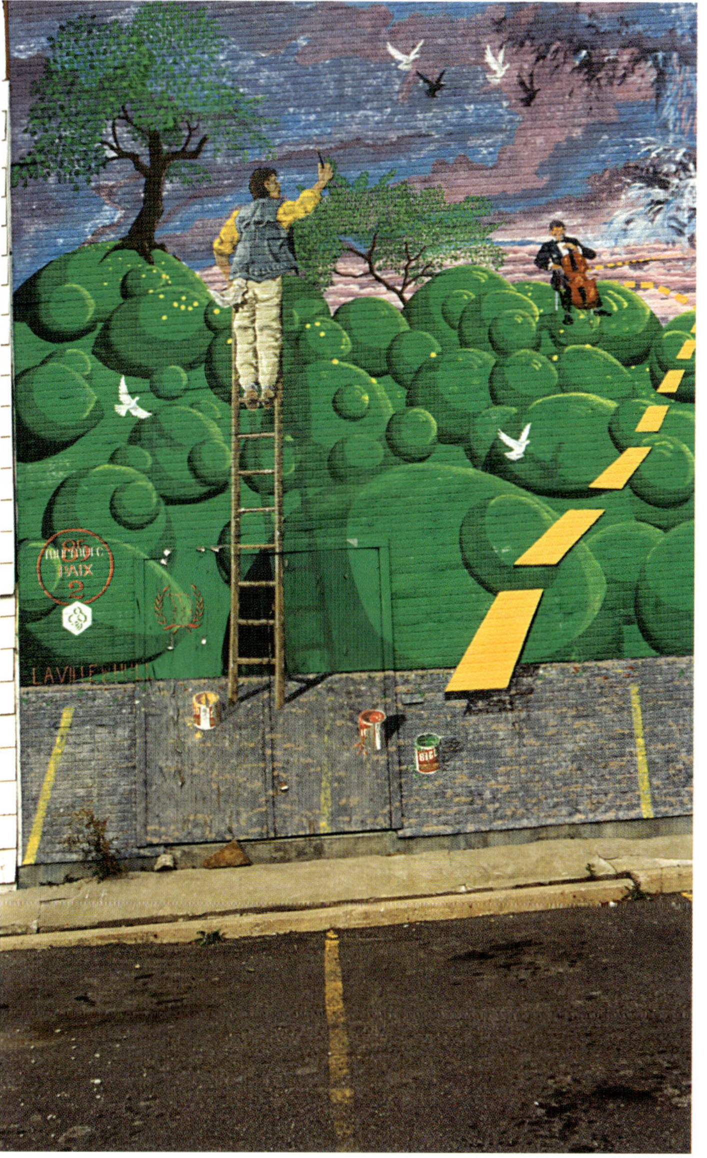
85
PAIX
2

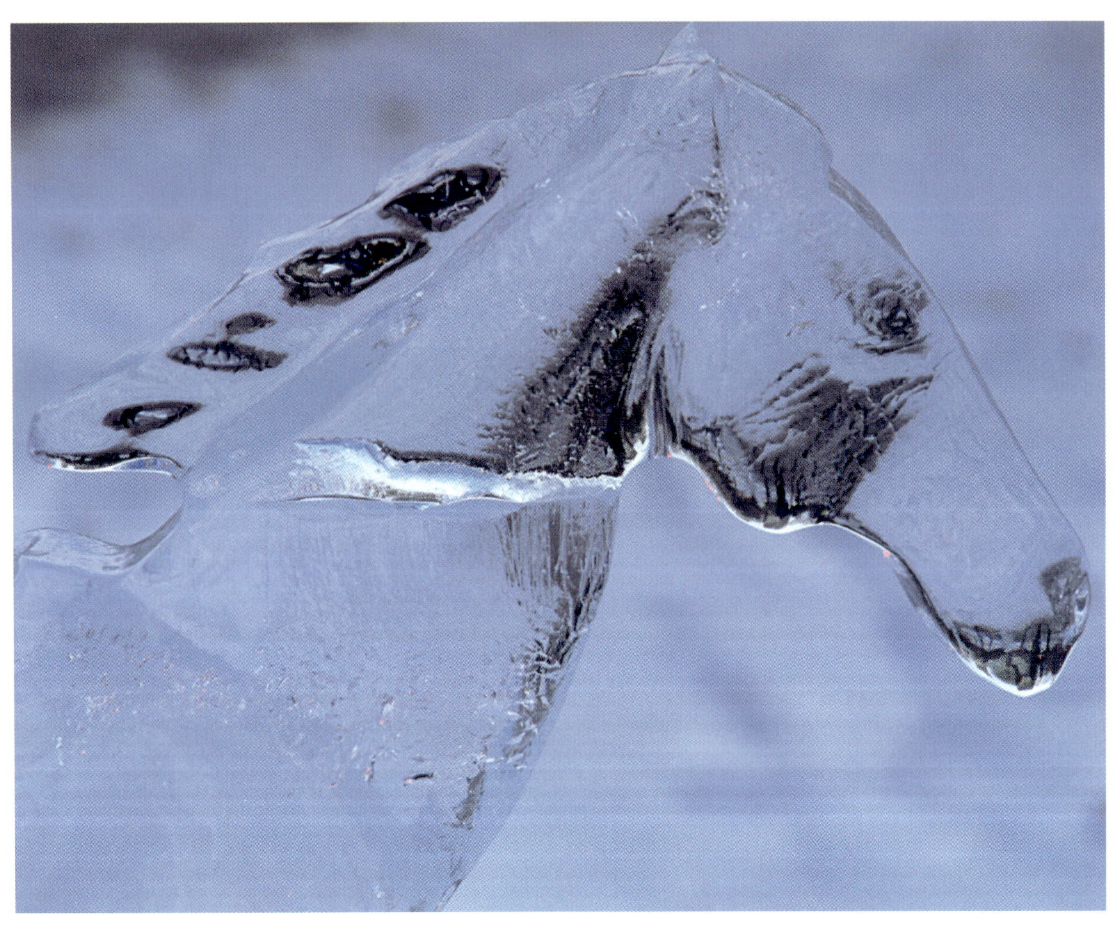

at full gallop
the ice steed in late-winter sun
starts to melt

spring sidewalk
and the crippled pencil vendor
is back

emerging
from melting snow — lumber
stacked by the recession

hazed in green
to their knees in flood
the willows bend

all night
the spring rain
soaking my dreams

off we go
all down the backroads
I & my little horse

floods subside
on shore the stonestacker
starts over

in the birdhouse hole
last year's straw
moves

having missed the bus
I walked
into spring

spring evening
from the antenna — a robin
pouring forth song

garbage cans
by moonlight seeming tipsy
and exuberantly full

a whiff of loam
and the sun on my neck
suddenly warm

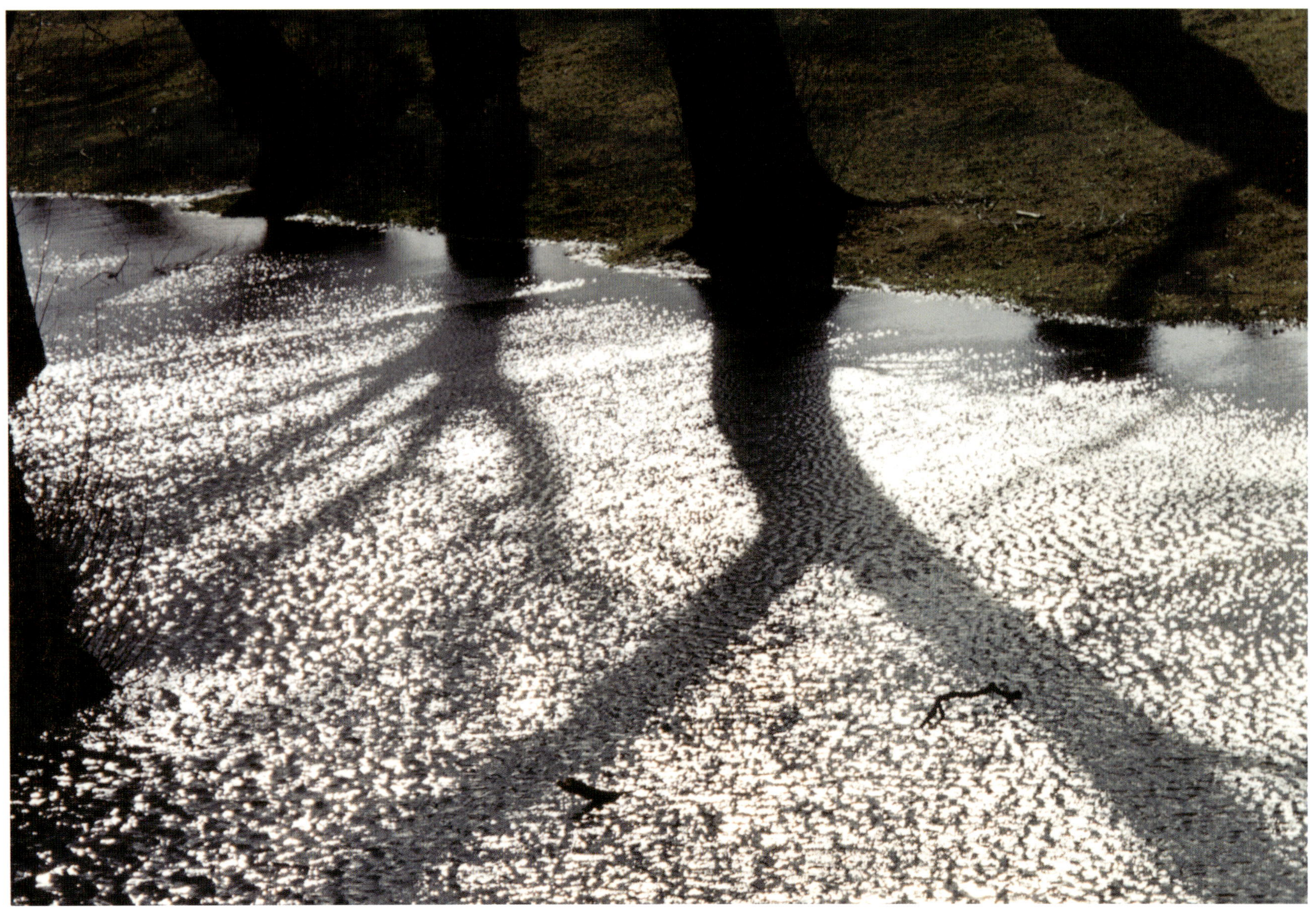

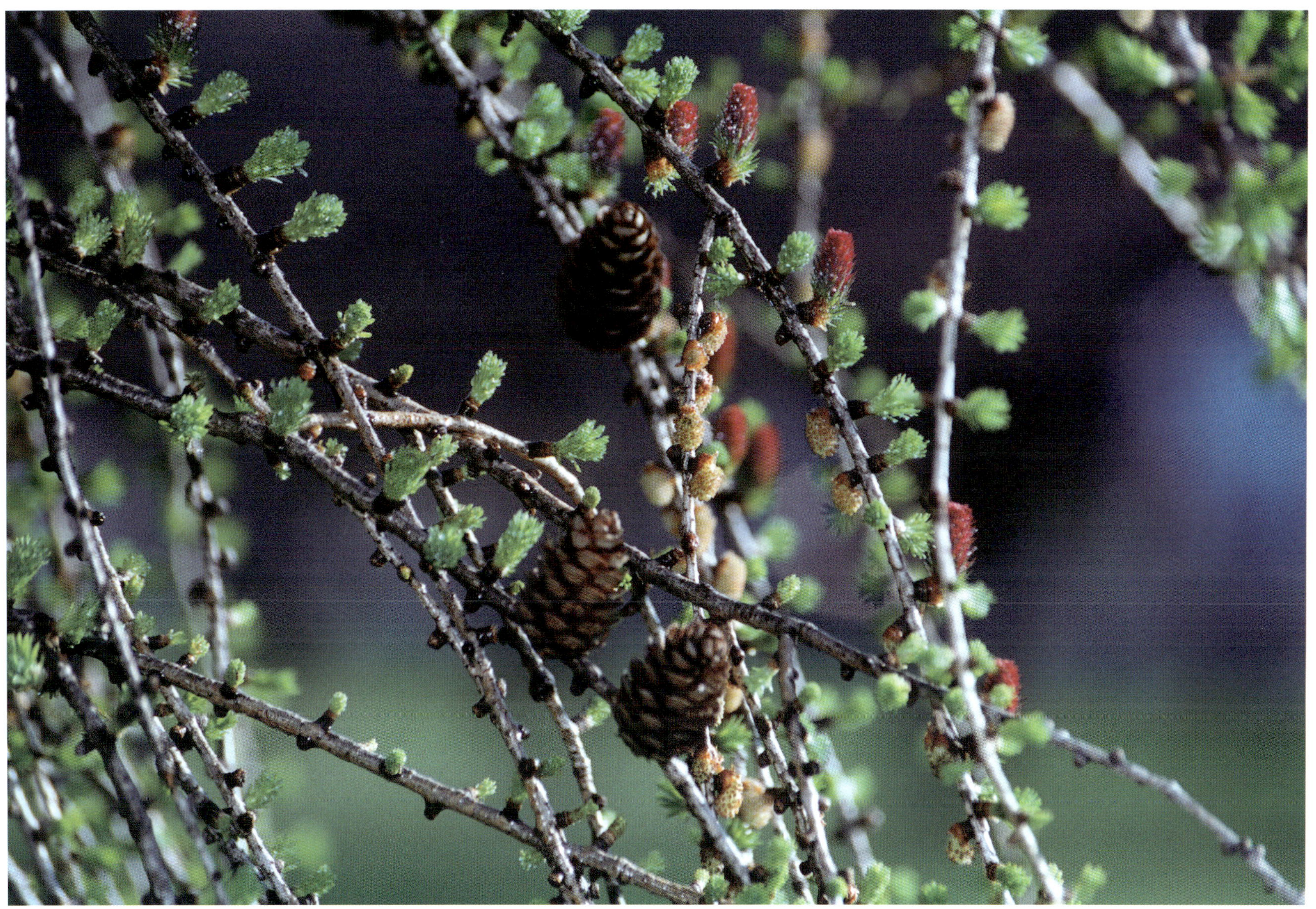

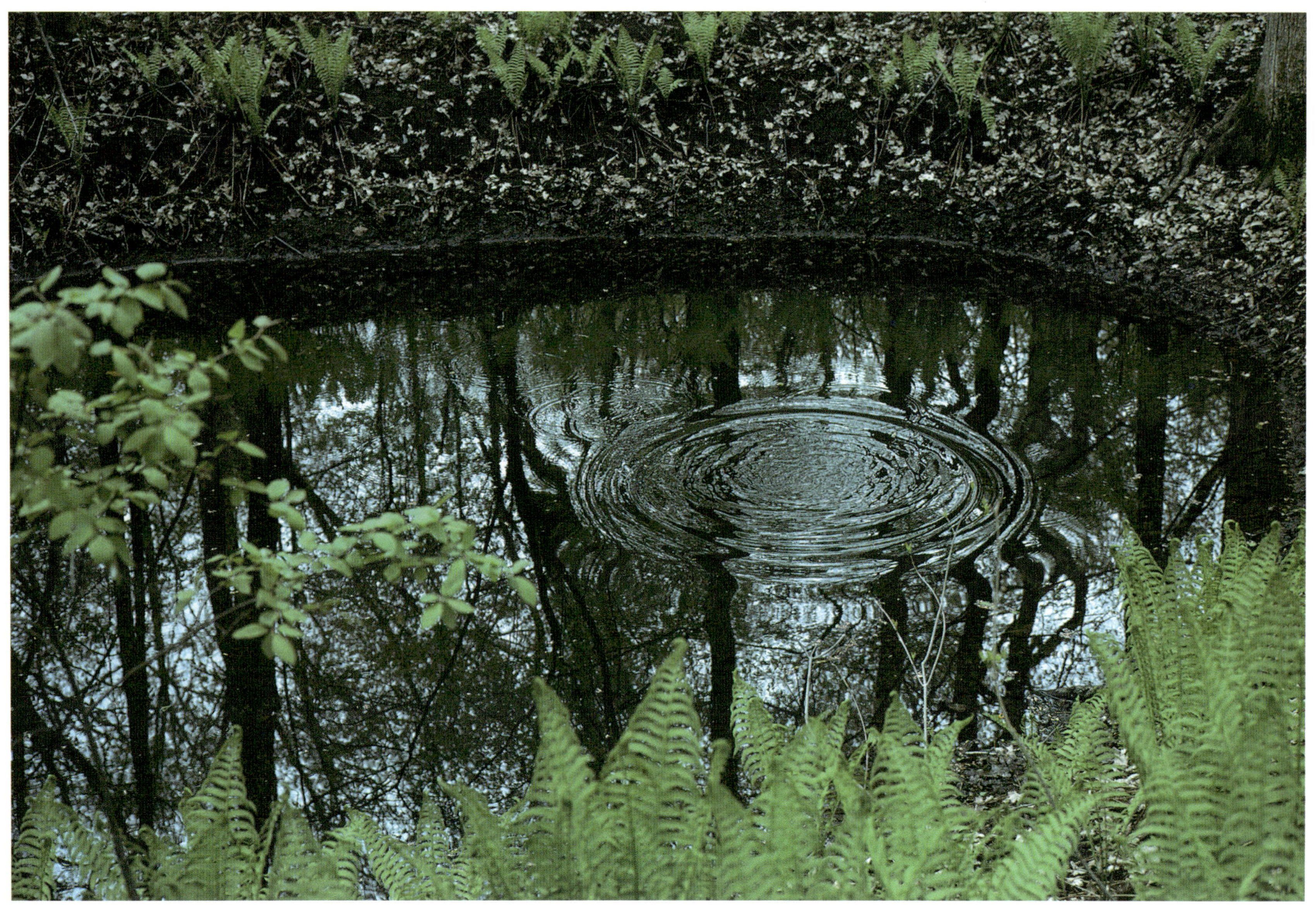

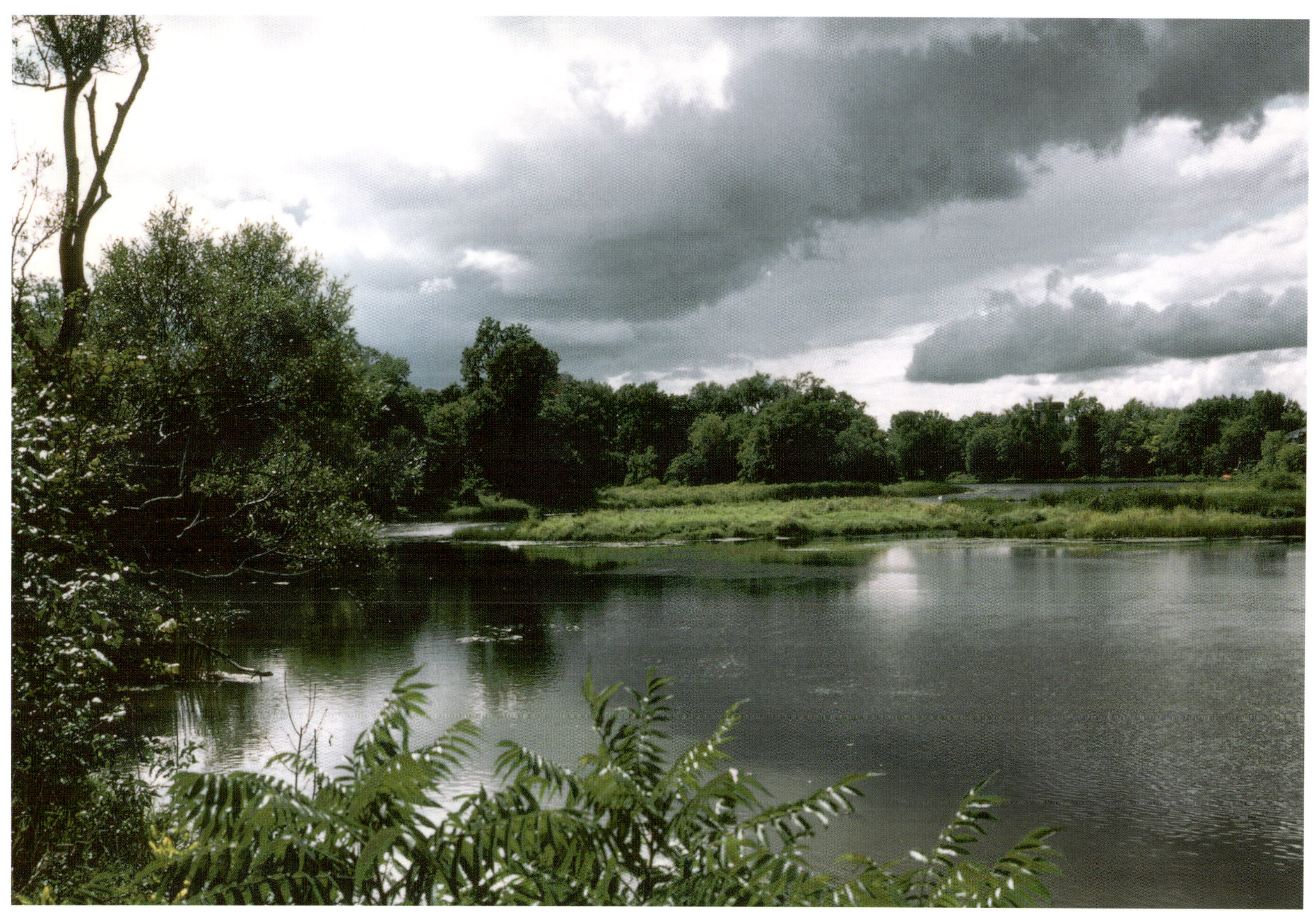

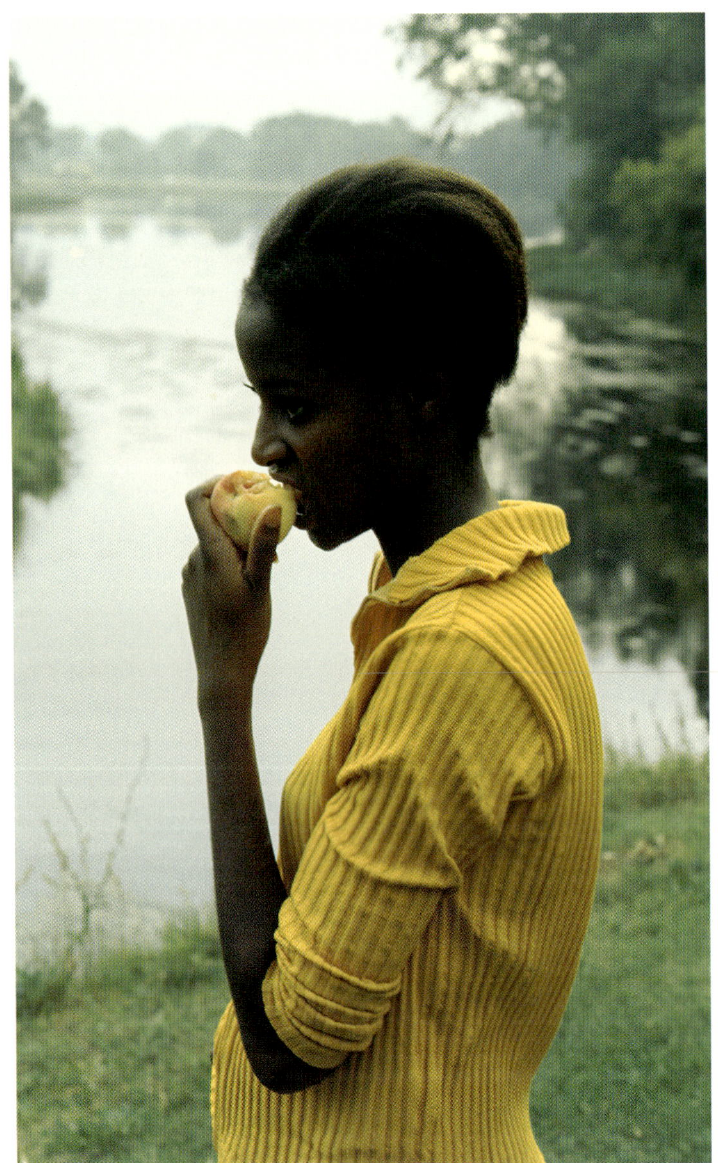

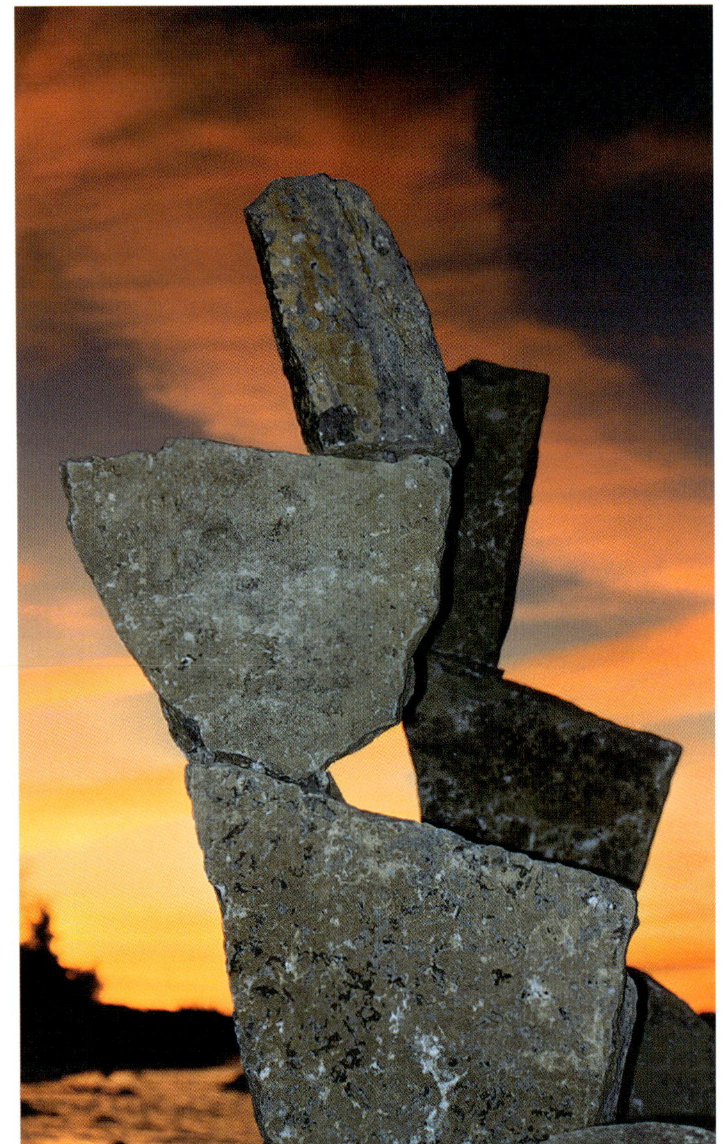

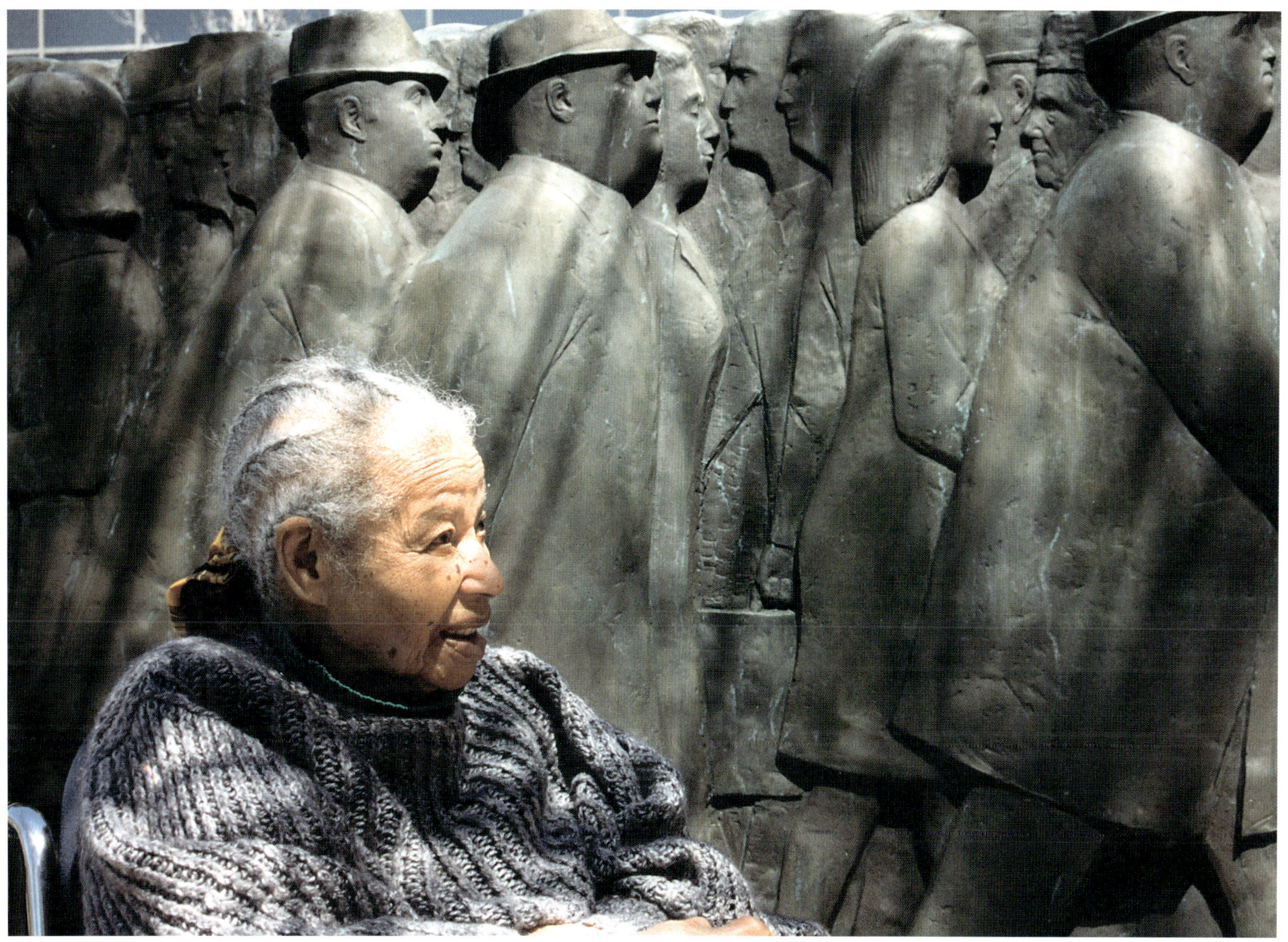

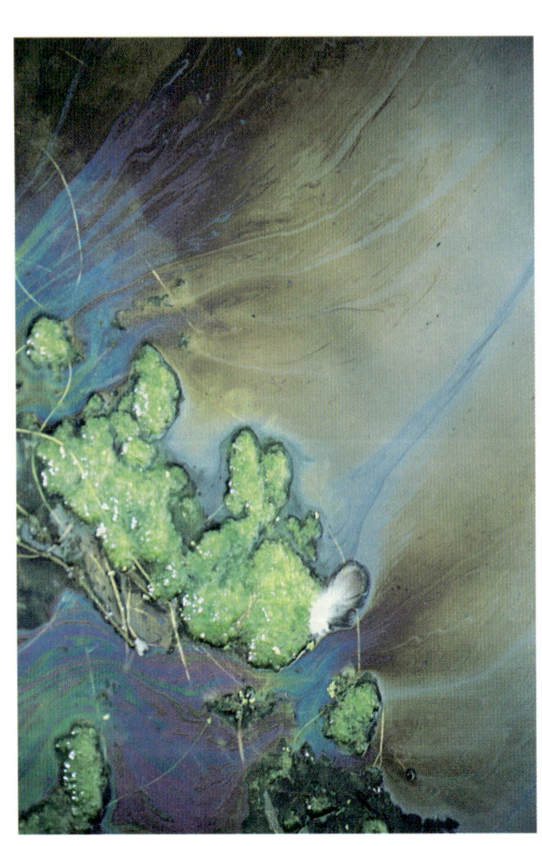

leaving home
feet first into mist
the local recluse

sleet
slashing red tulips
— the phone rings

o ragged crow
that rasping shout
must hurt your throat

planting lettuce
as our bedsheets billow
softly in the sun

gently
on every leaf
rain

thunder
rattling
a pane of clouds

after the call
for comfort — I curl
on his side of the bed

the moving-van leaves
apple petals swirling
over the drive

in a rusty bucket
rainwater
sunset

dawn
is rinsing
the stars away

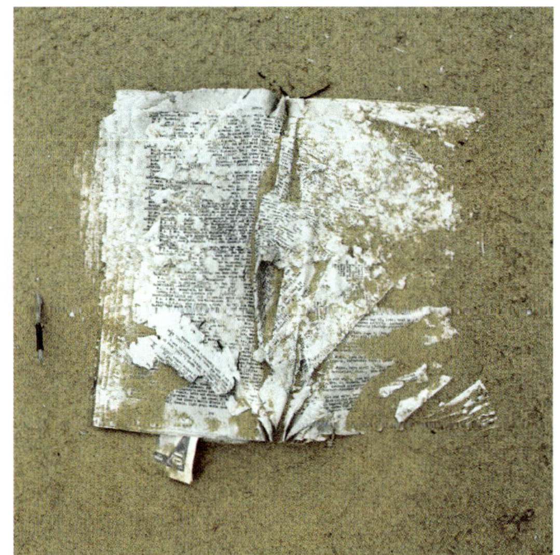

we used to shriek
at tag like that — unaware
it grows dark

behind the church
discarded lilies
in the morning sun

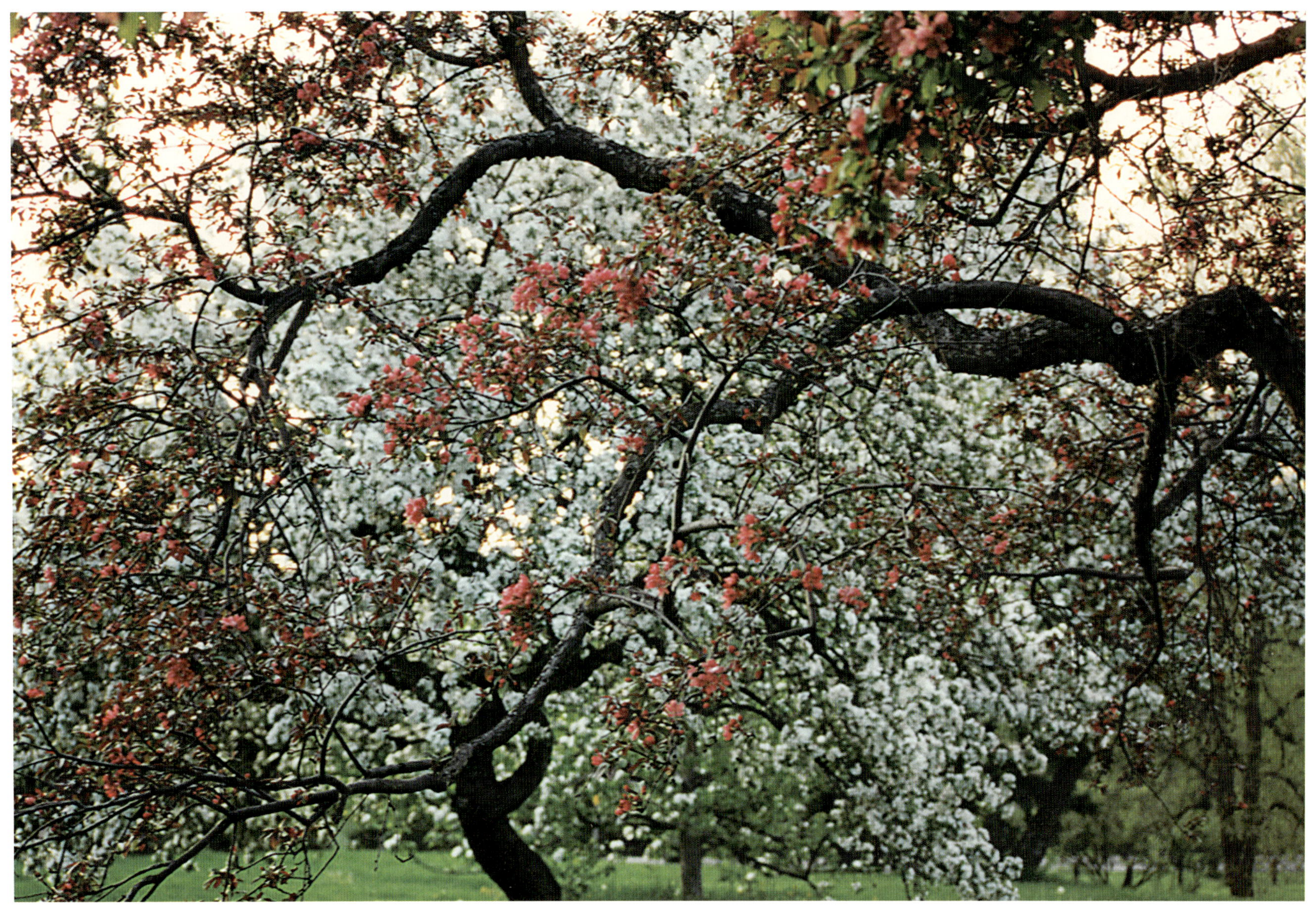

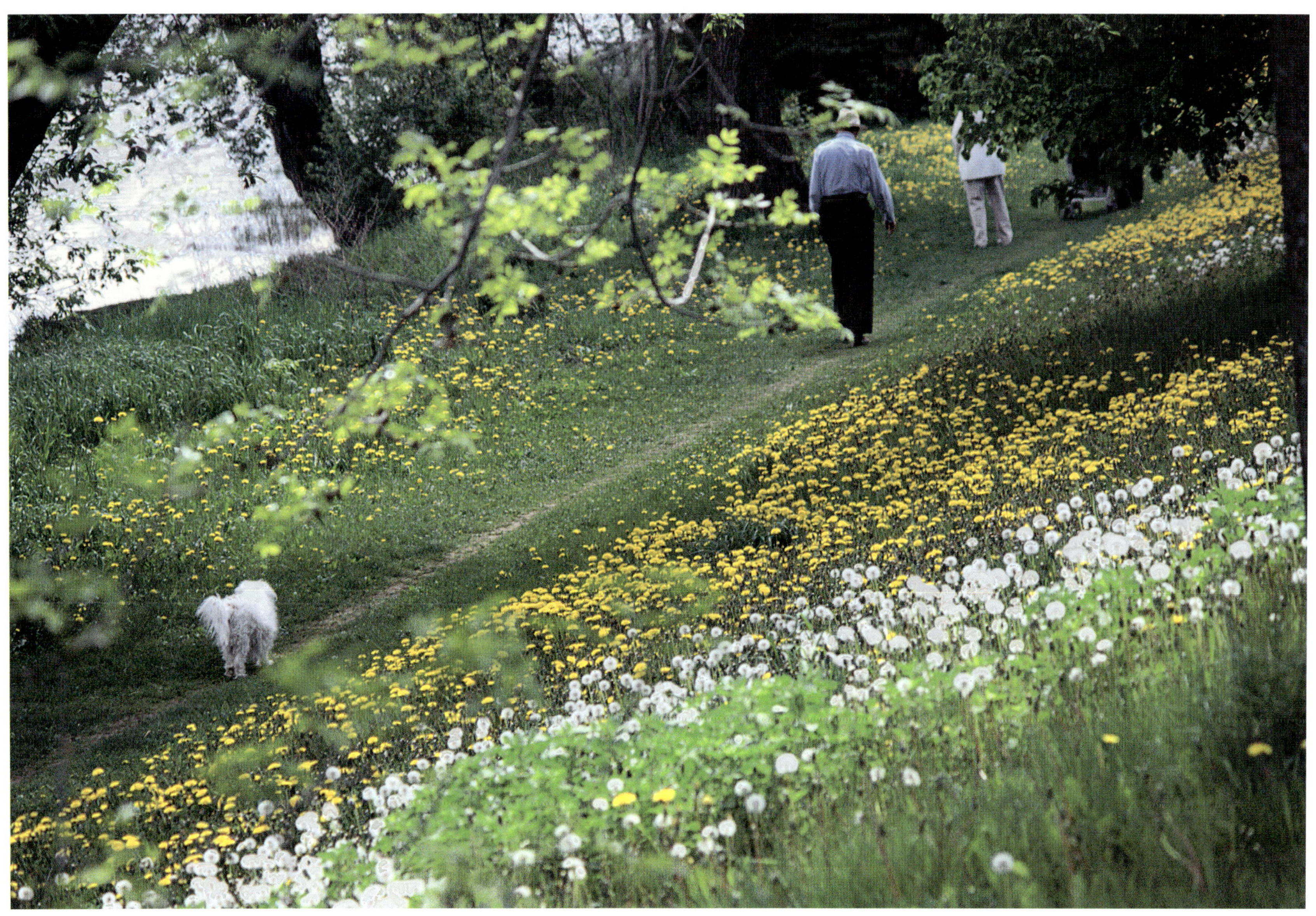

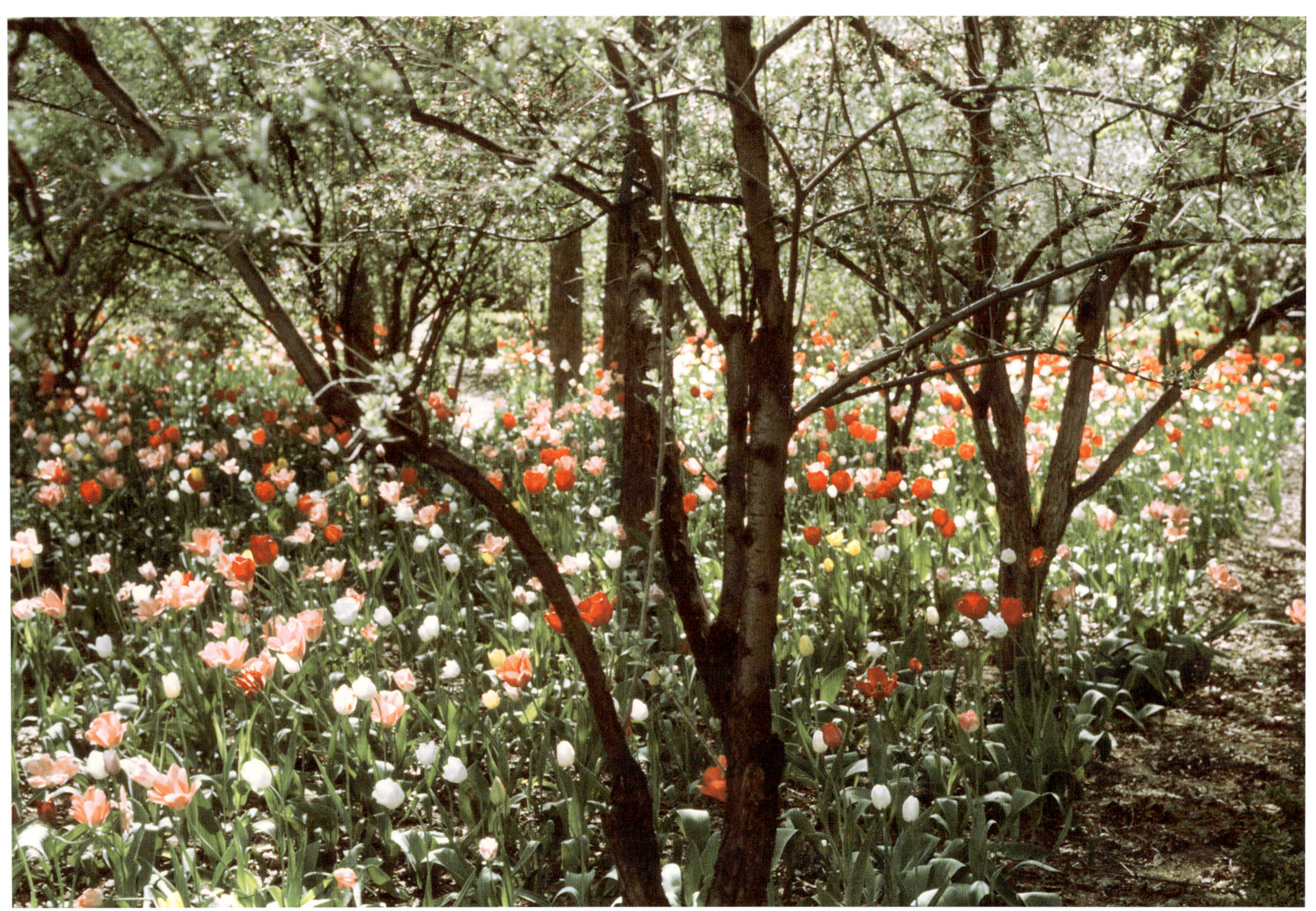

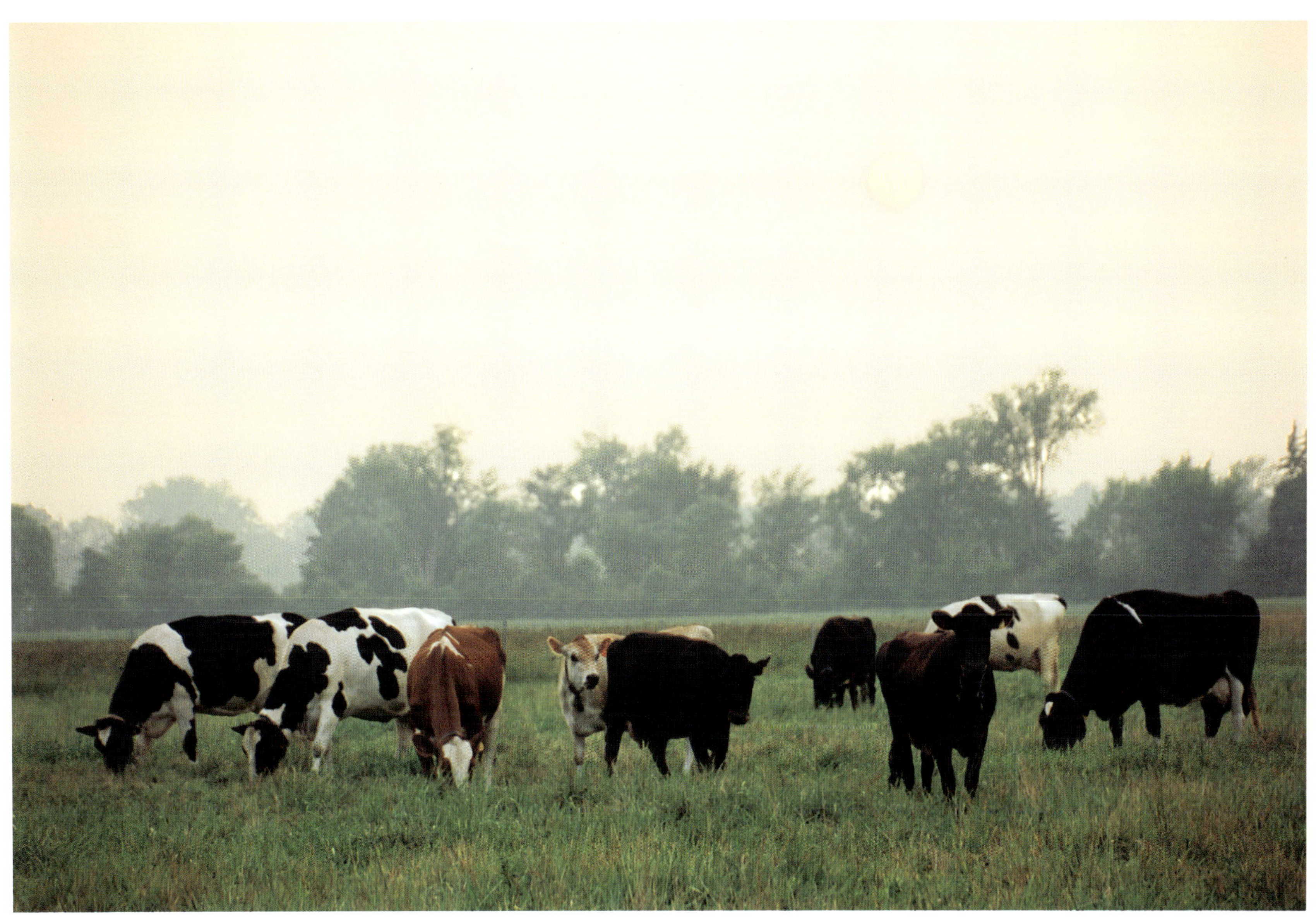

Early Evening Pieces

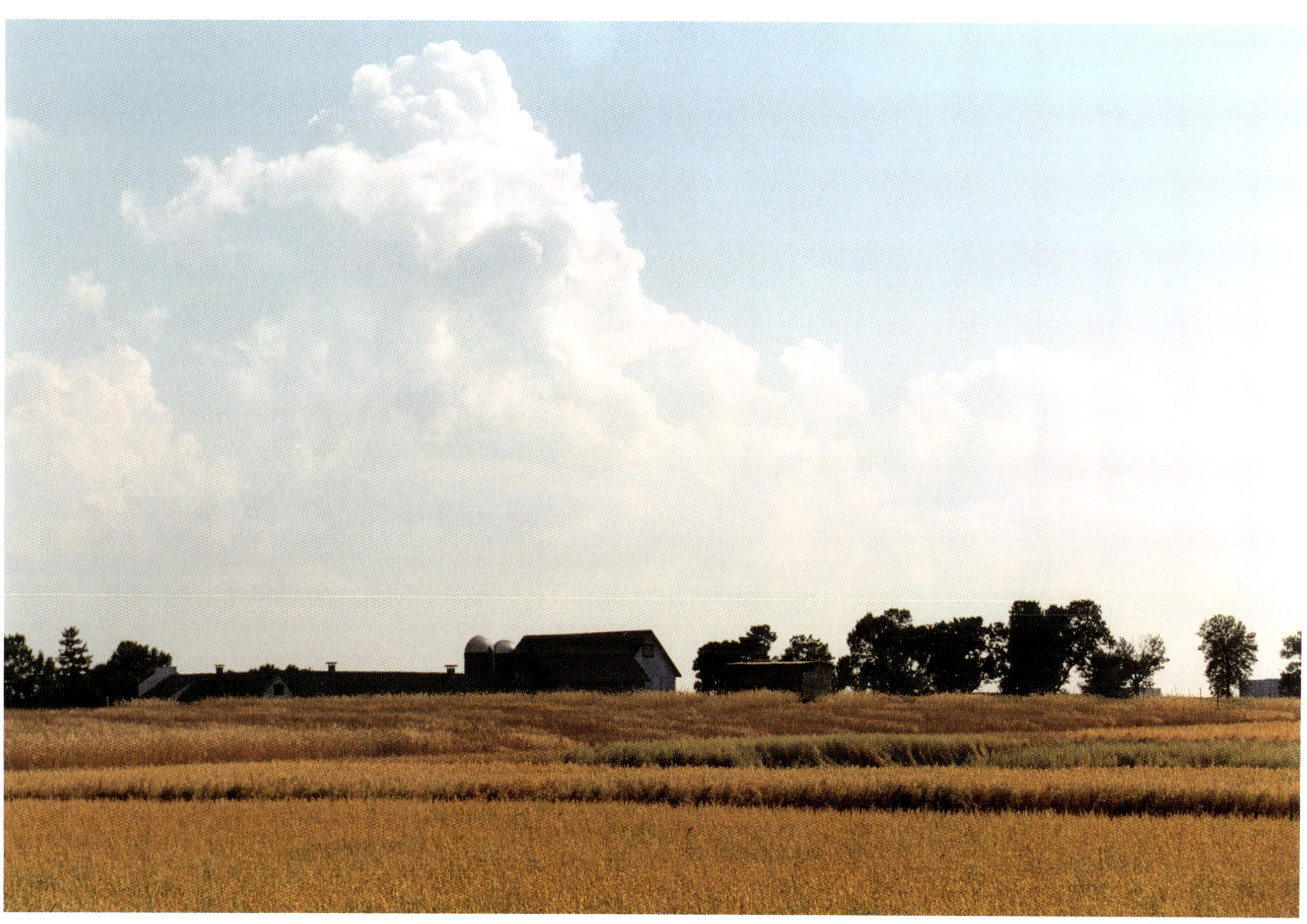

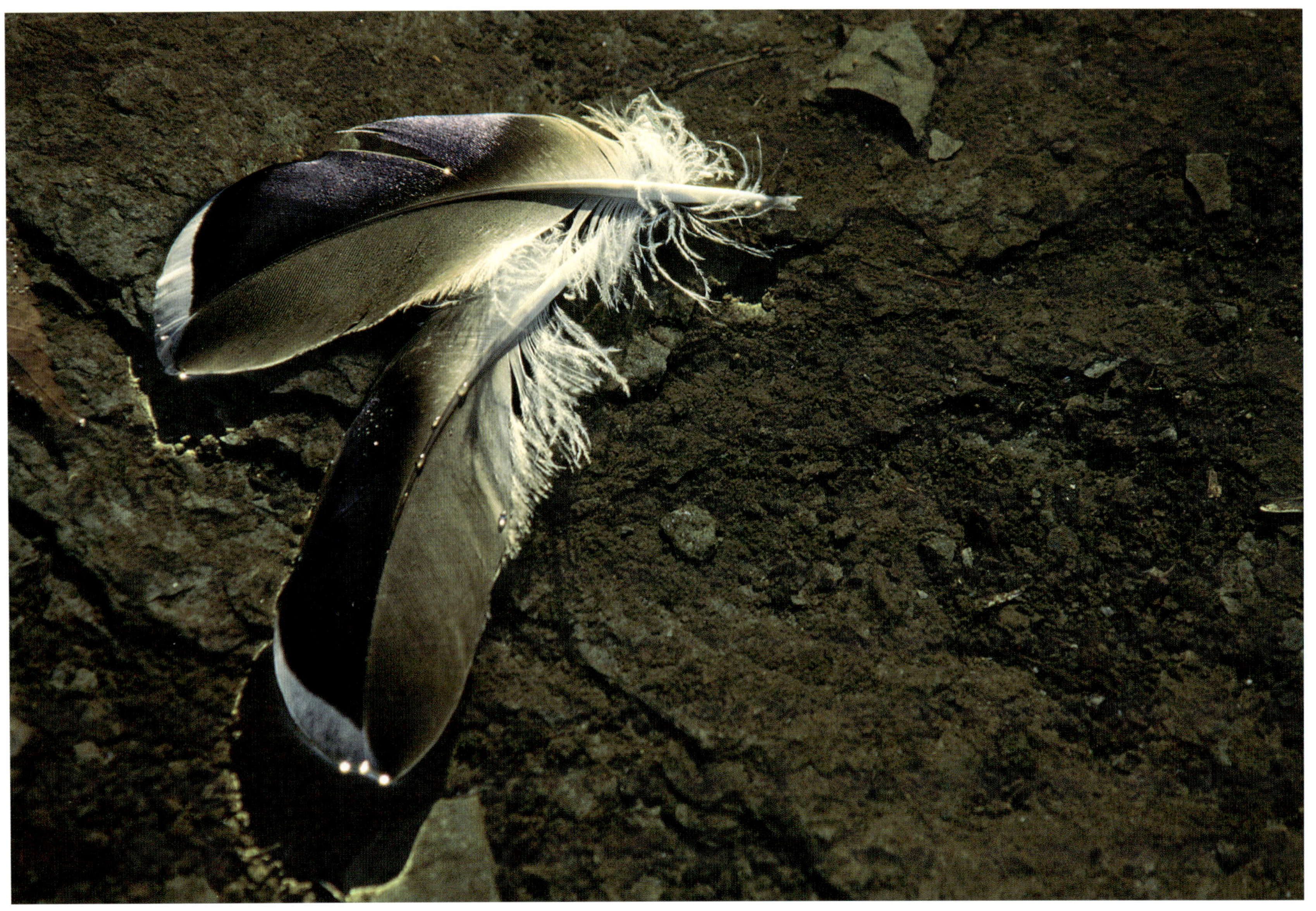

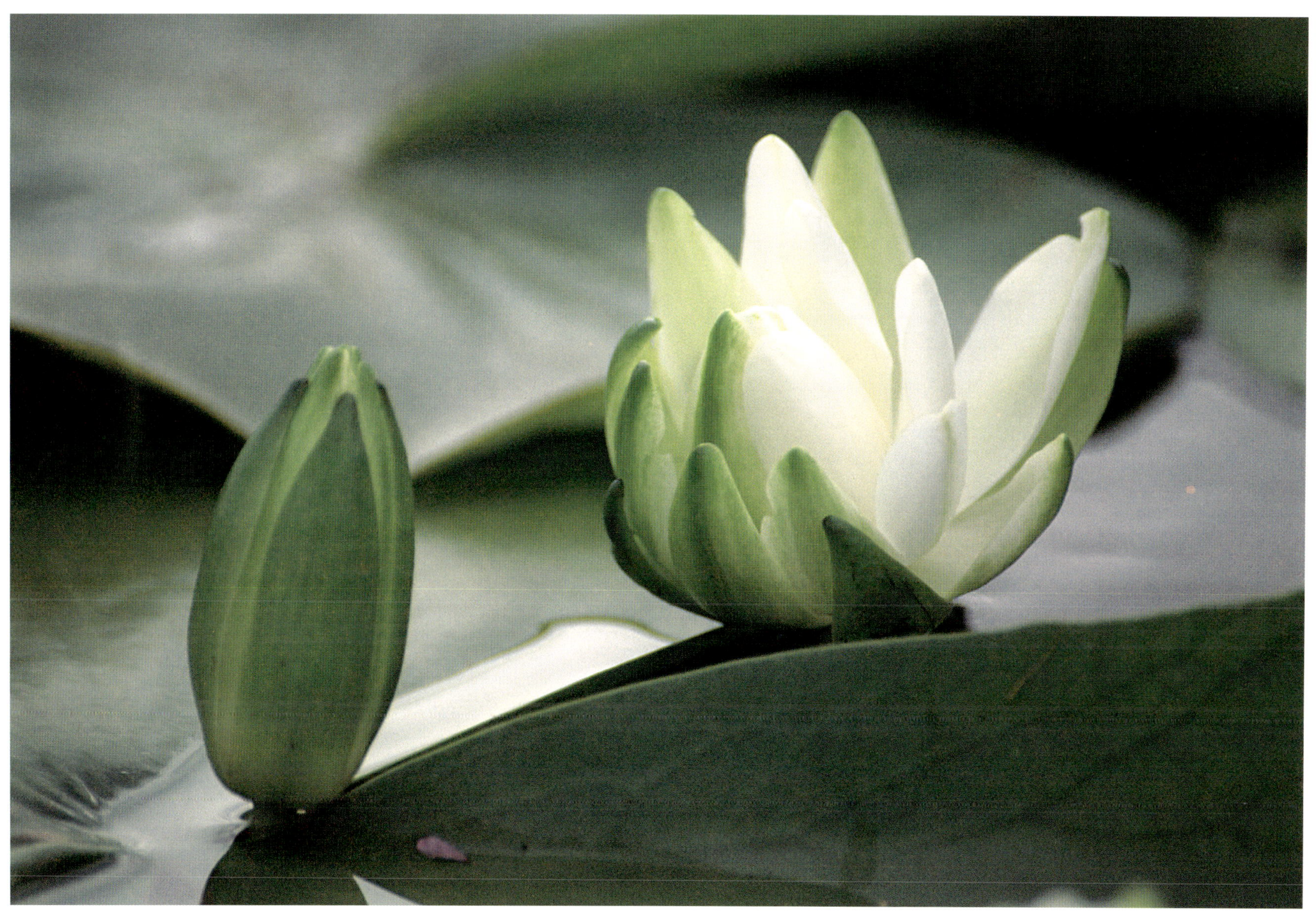

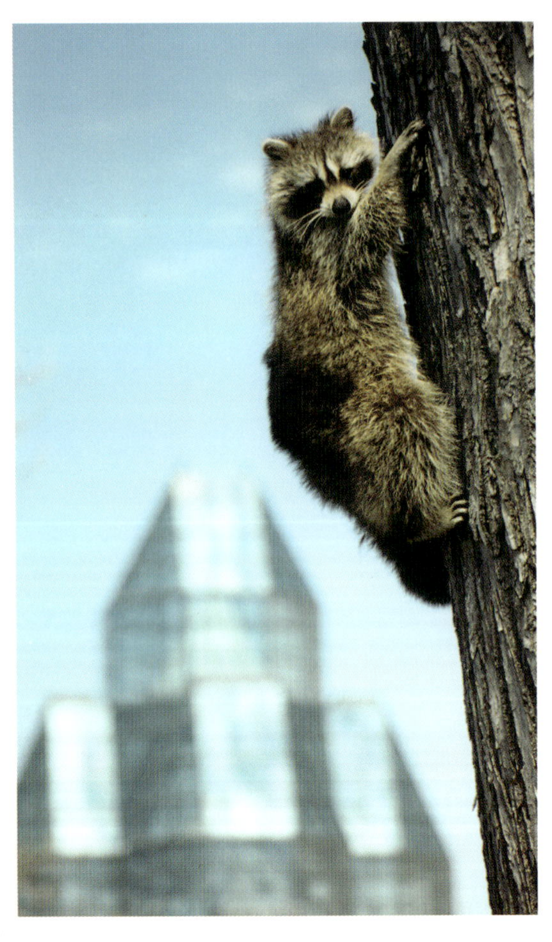

spirea
the wind loosens
confetti ...

except for Brahms
in the kitchen
no one

midnight
the hibachi
still glowing

hot winds
under hydro pylons
the long grass sings

as I enter the antique shop
the bell of the owner's cat
tinkles

with one foot out
a child considers
the moving-stairs

supper alone
letting the cat
lick my plate

leaning on a maple
the lineman in his hardhat
peels an egg

a heat bug drones
under gauze
the baby frets

my high beams
on a long curve hitting
tombstones

with his hand on my thigh
& thunder grinding
the heatwave ends

into the river's
dawn haze — that red canoe
has disappeared

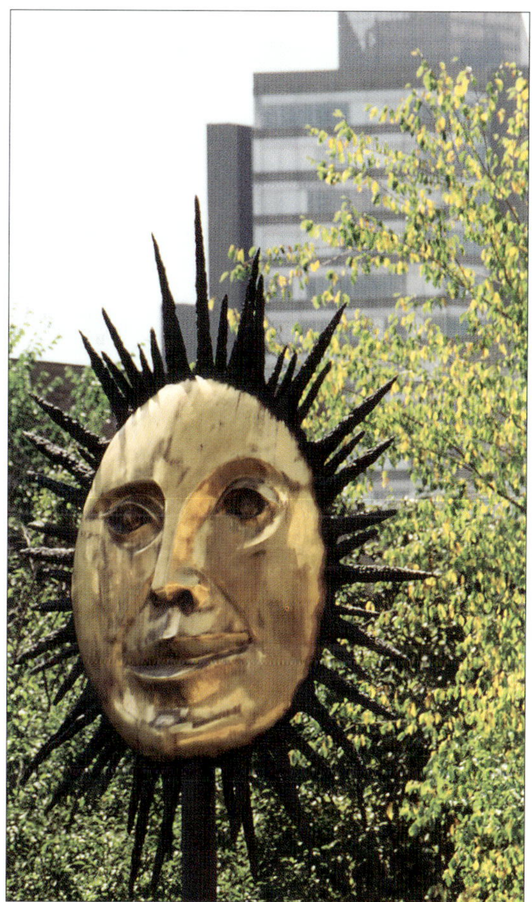

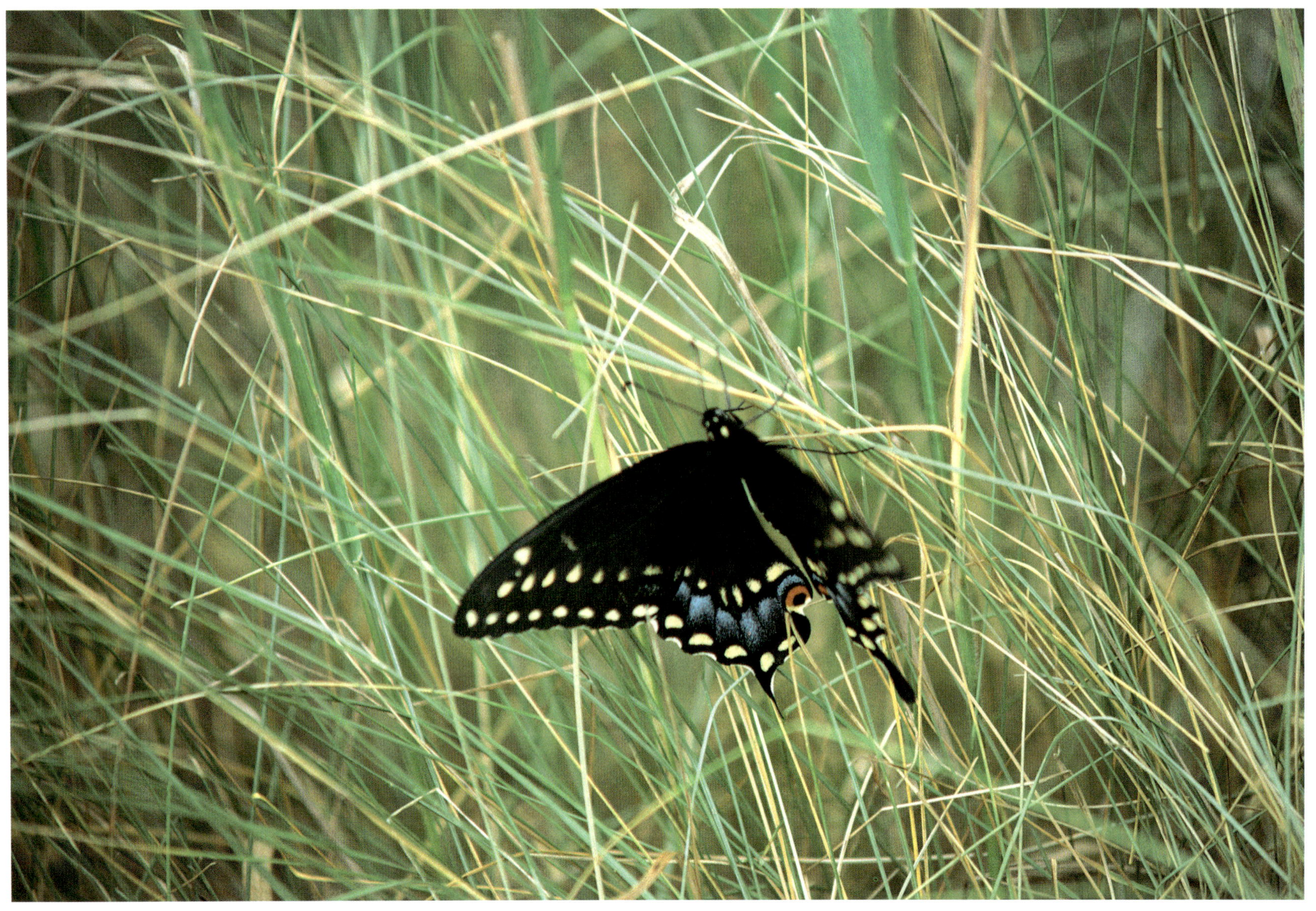

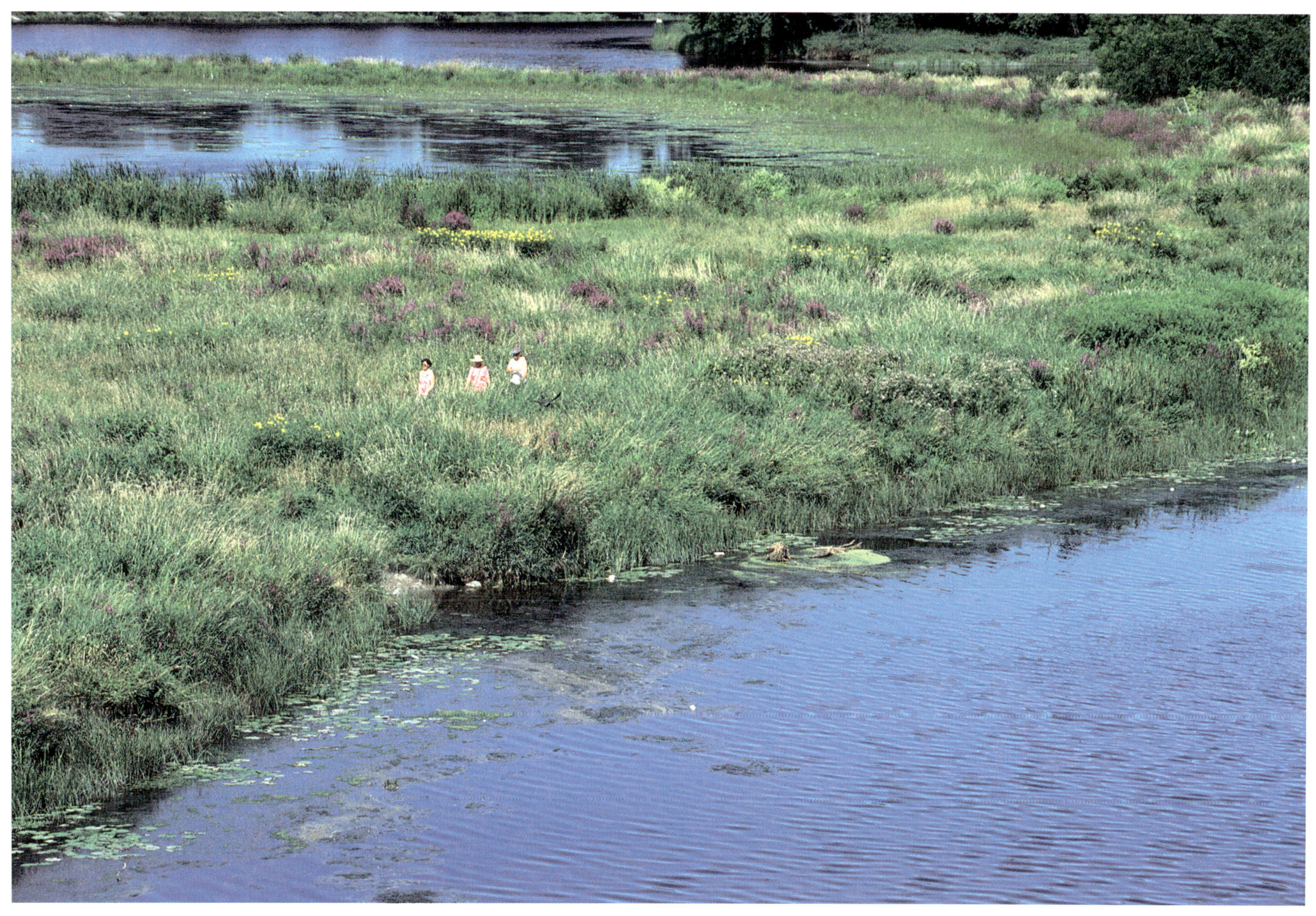

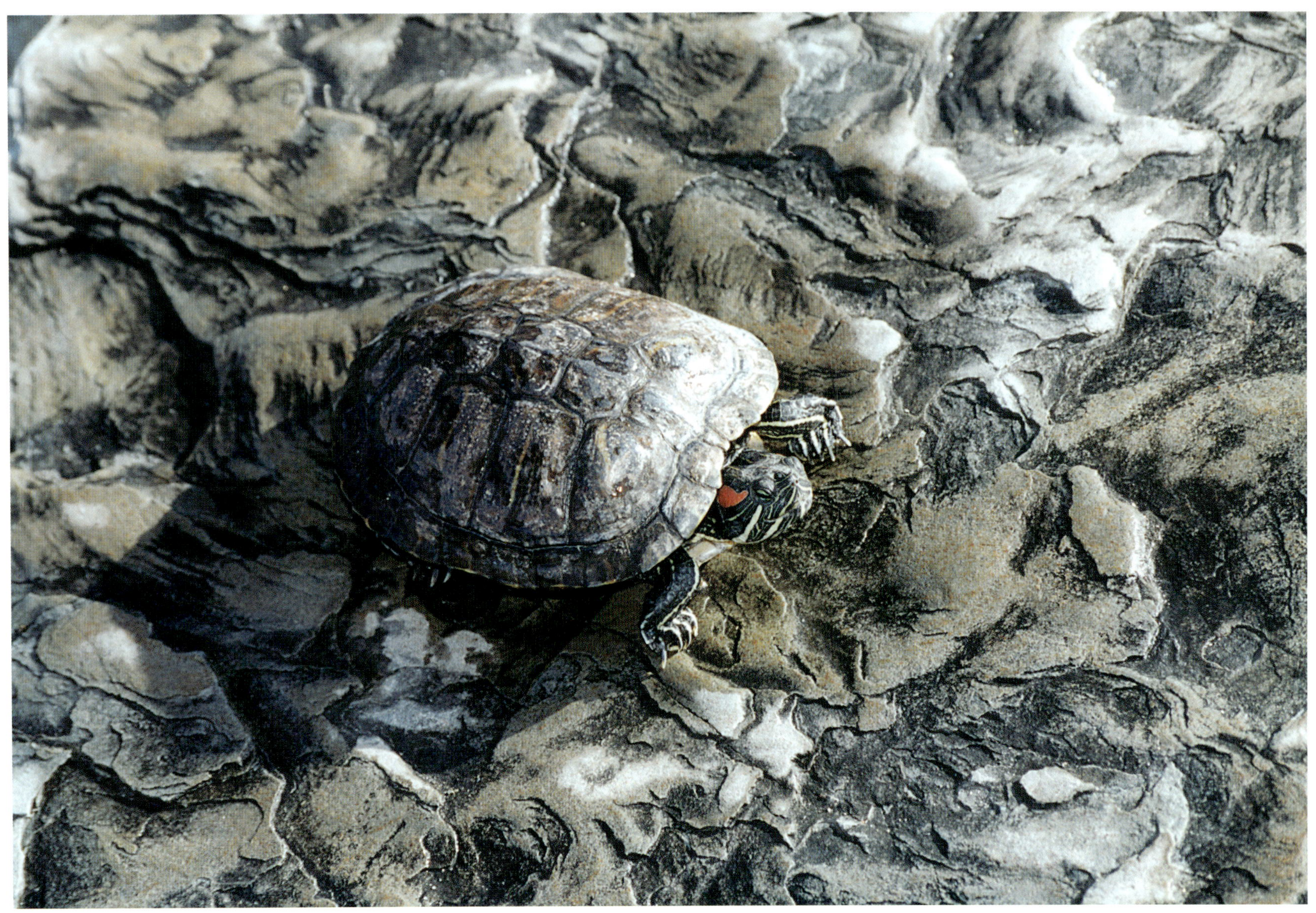

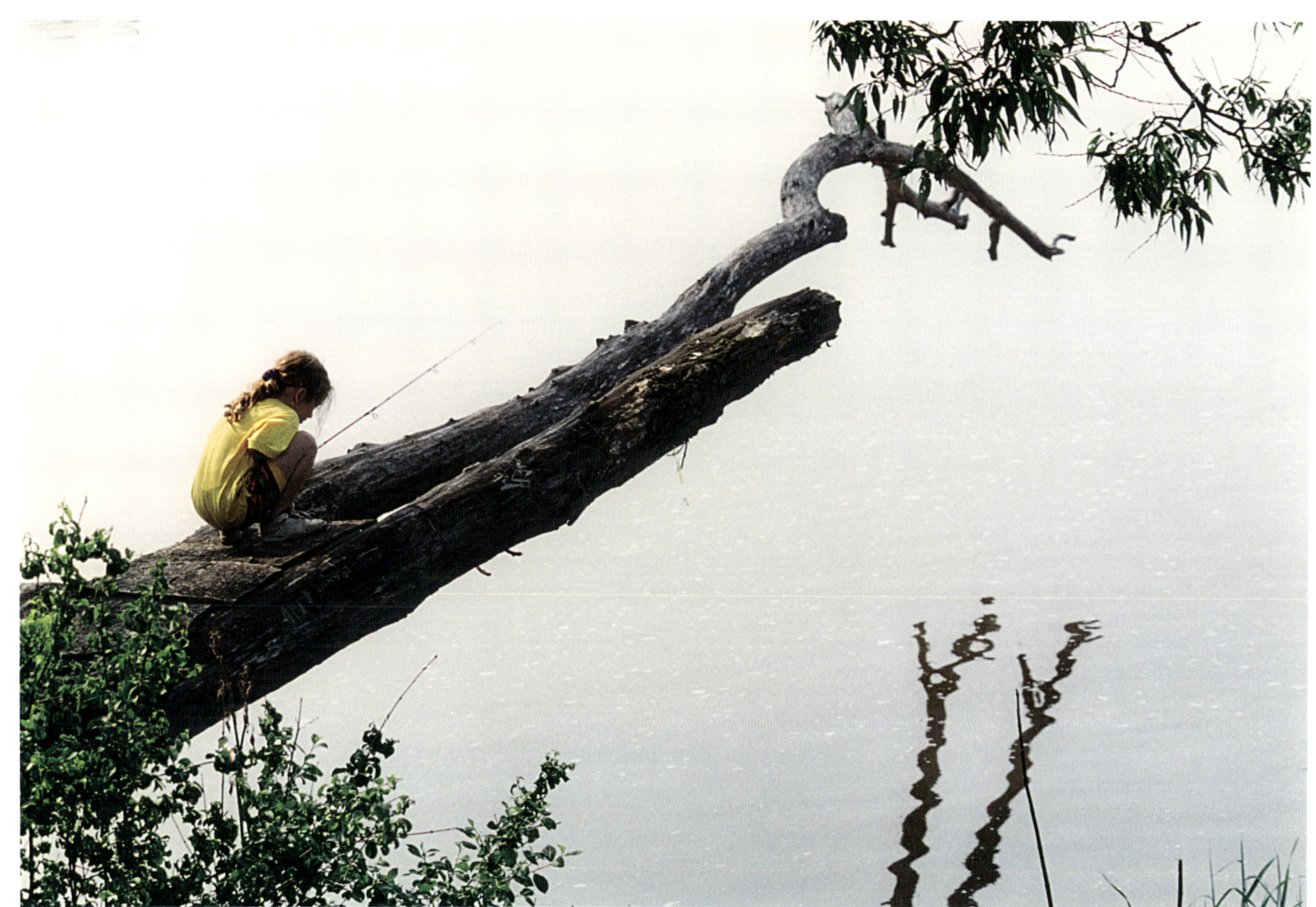

one loon calls
across the lake
— a light

the sun goes down
gliding by the cliff — a raven
meets its shadow

the lake darkens
harder and harder
the empty rowboat rocks

lightning
& something small
streaks into the woodpile

through the reeds
moonlight silvering
a path for my canoe

in the burnt forest
one branch of green
non-surrender

a breeze
through wisteria lifting
hairs on his chest

below the dam
boulder shadows lengthen
on cracked mud

skin to skin
open mouthed
in the warm night rain

rolling over the hayfields
clouds
and cloud shadows

legs adangle
on swings — three children
turn their ice-creams

shuffling home
at twilight — the veteran
with bones for his dog

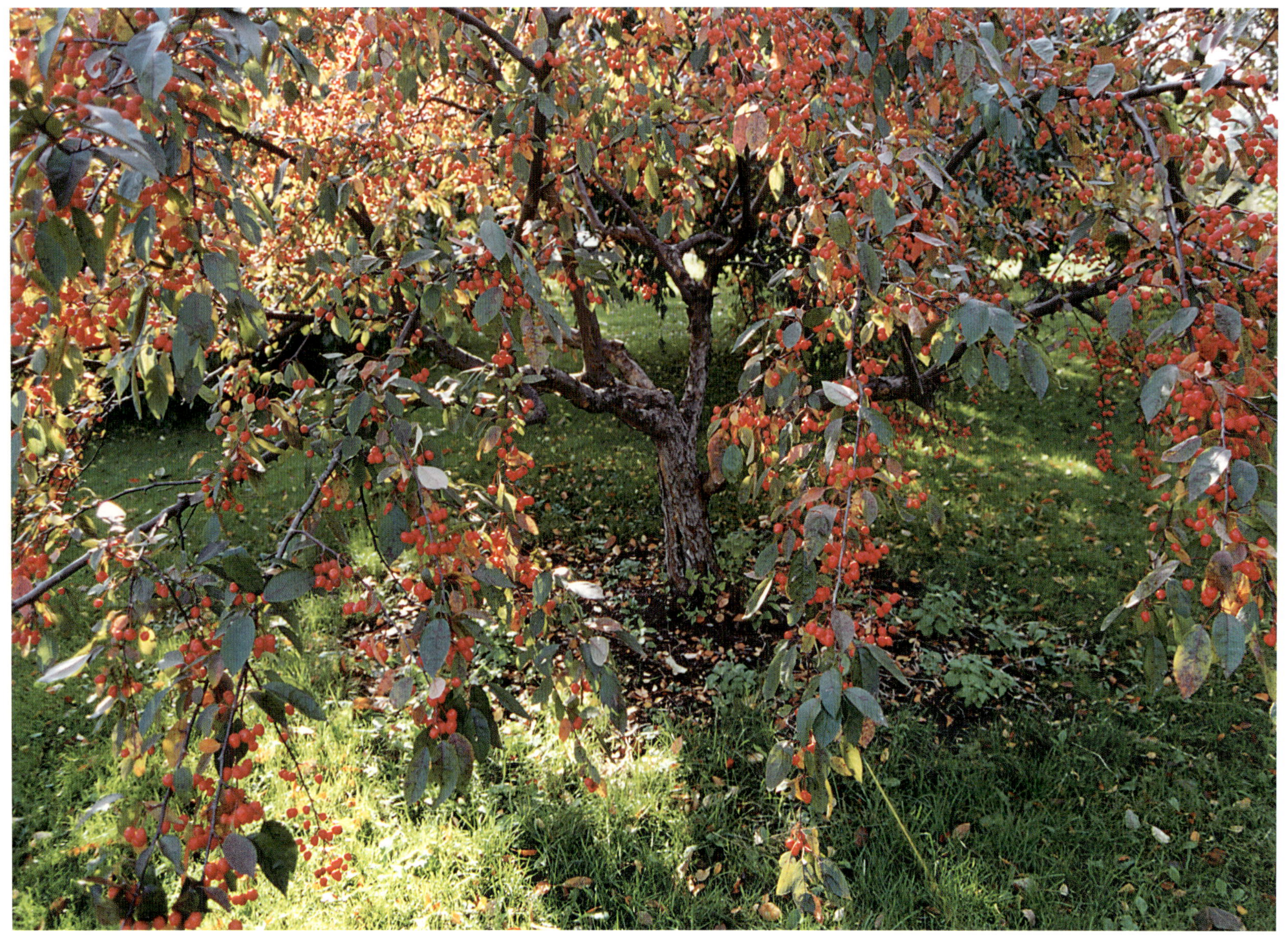

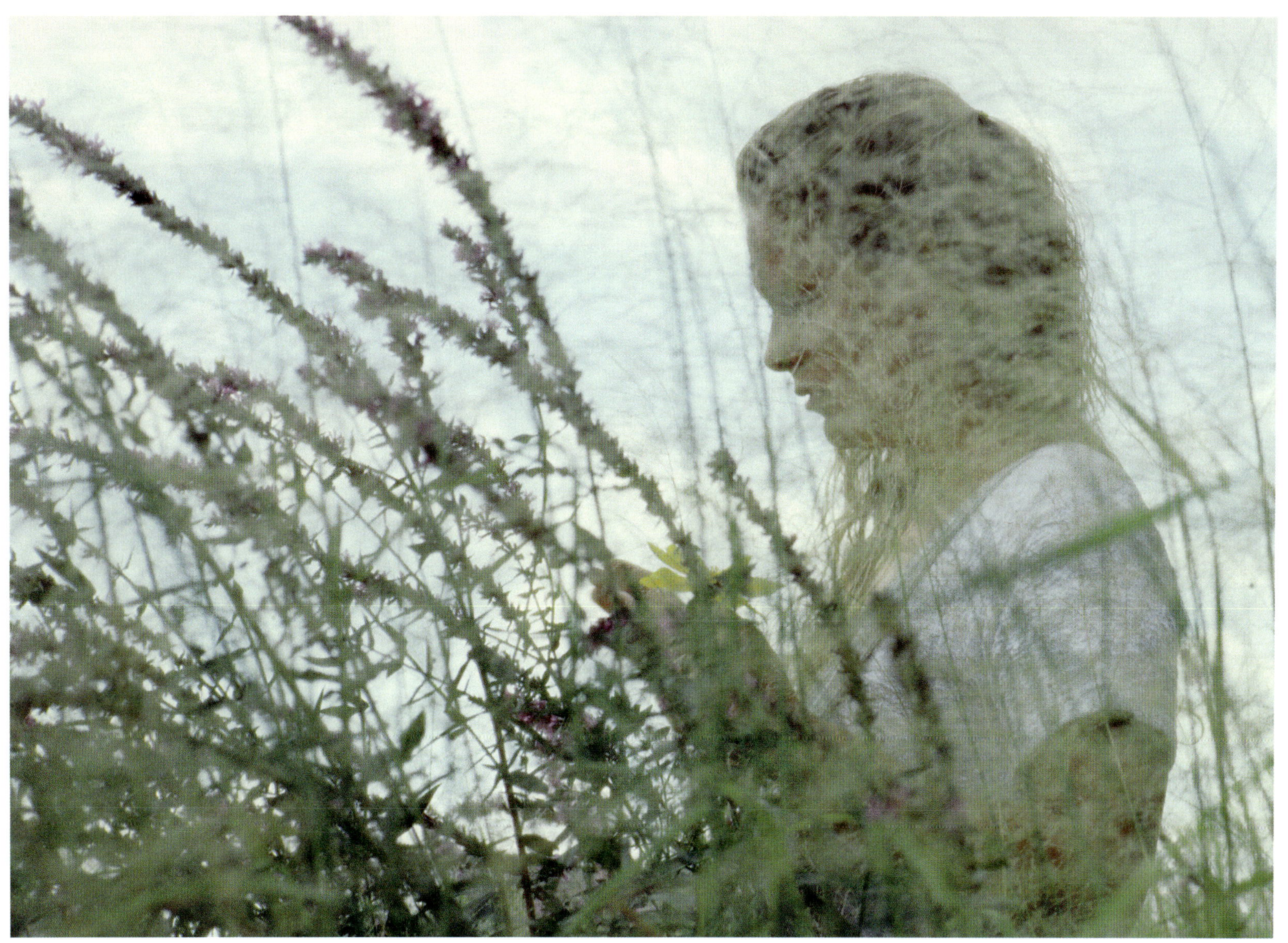

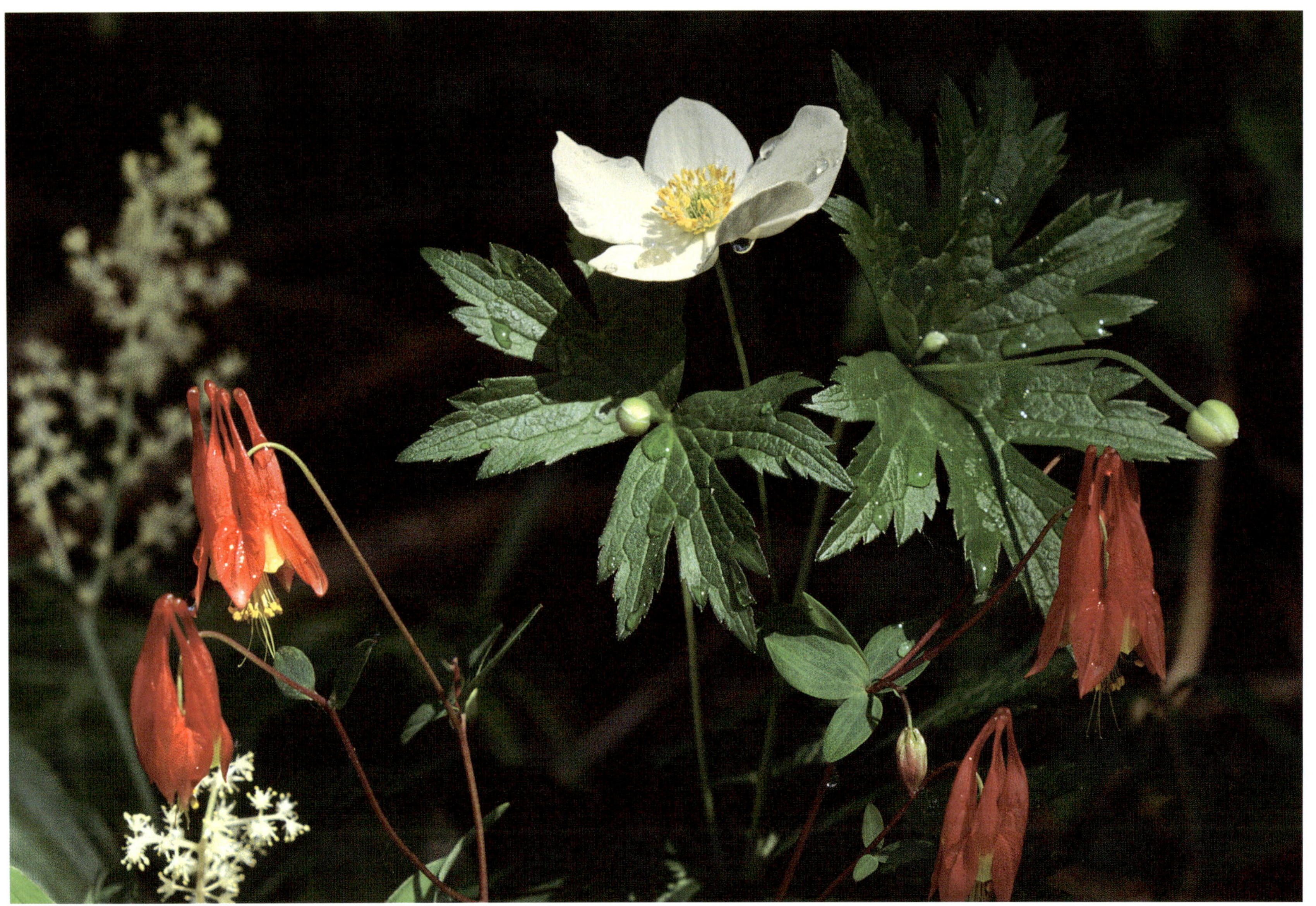

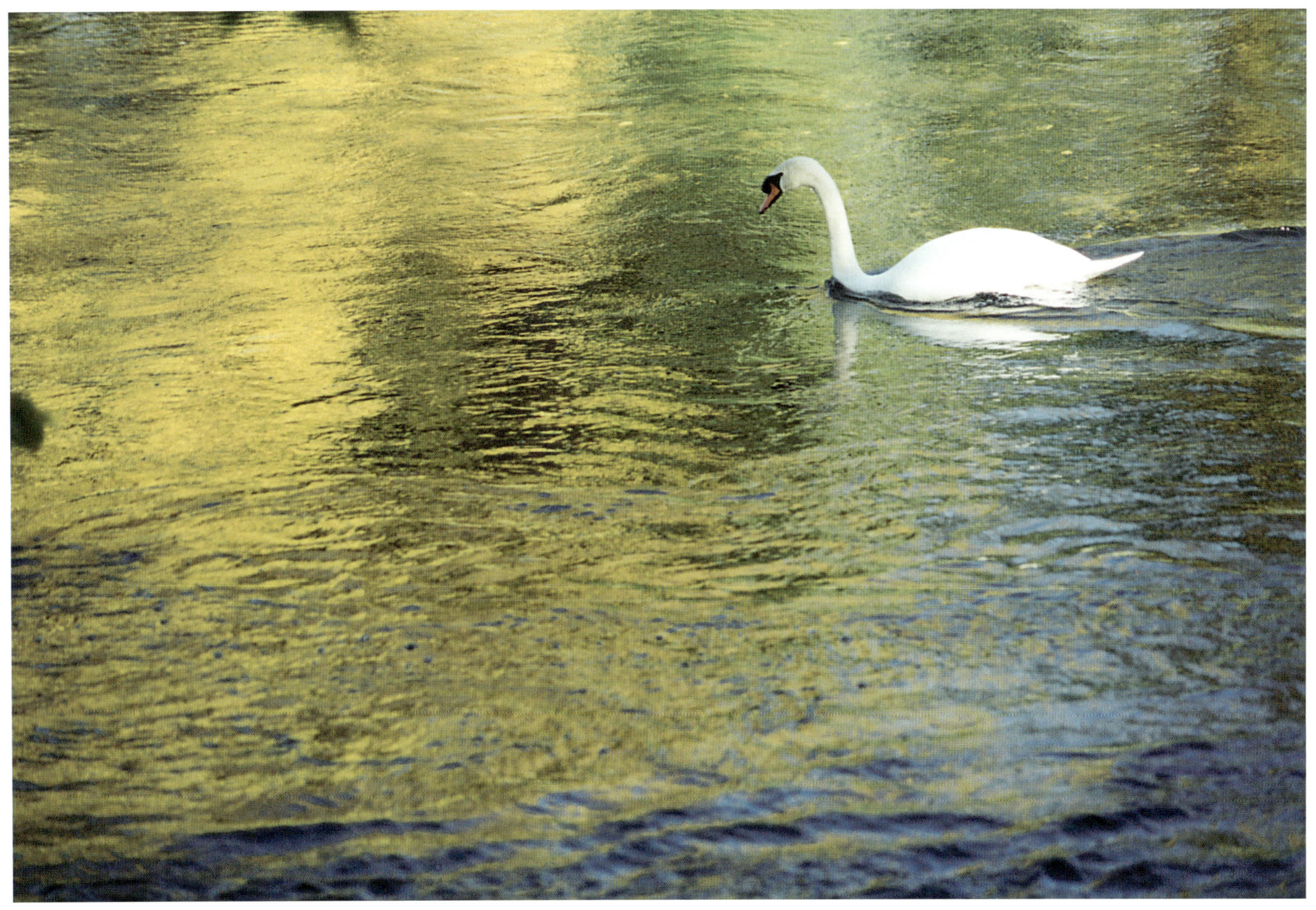

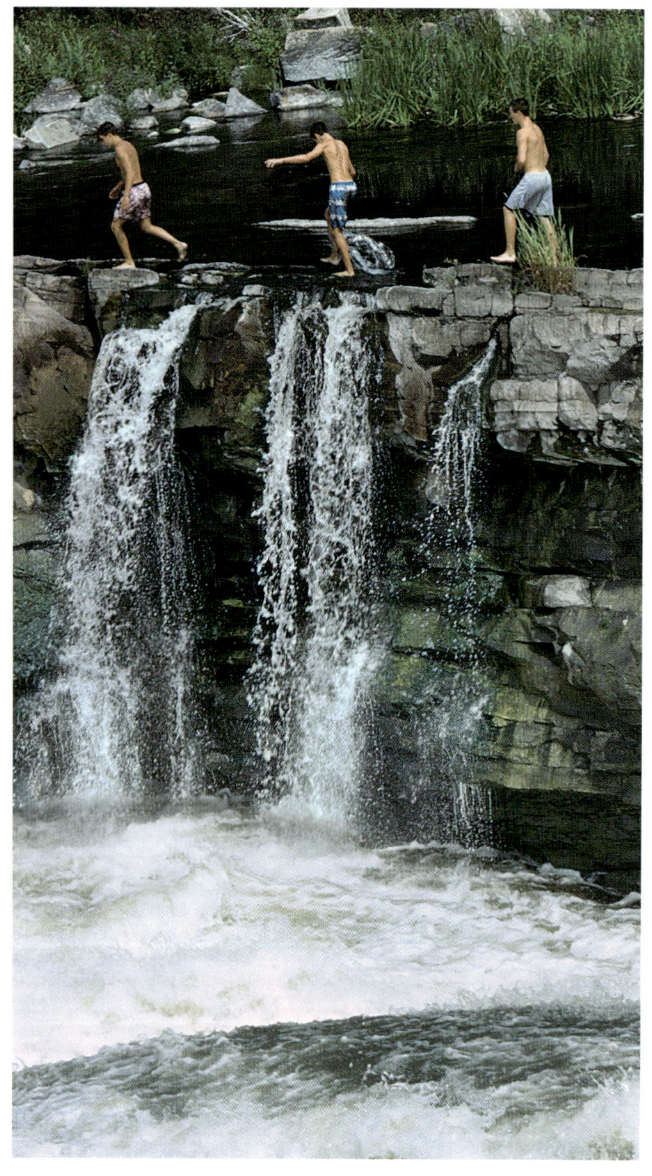

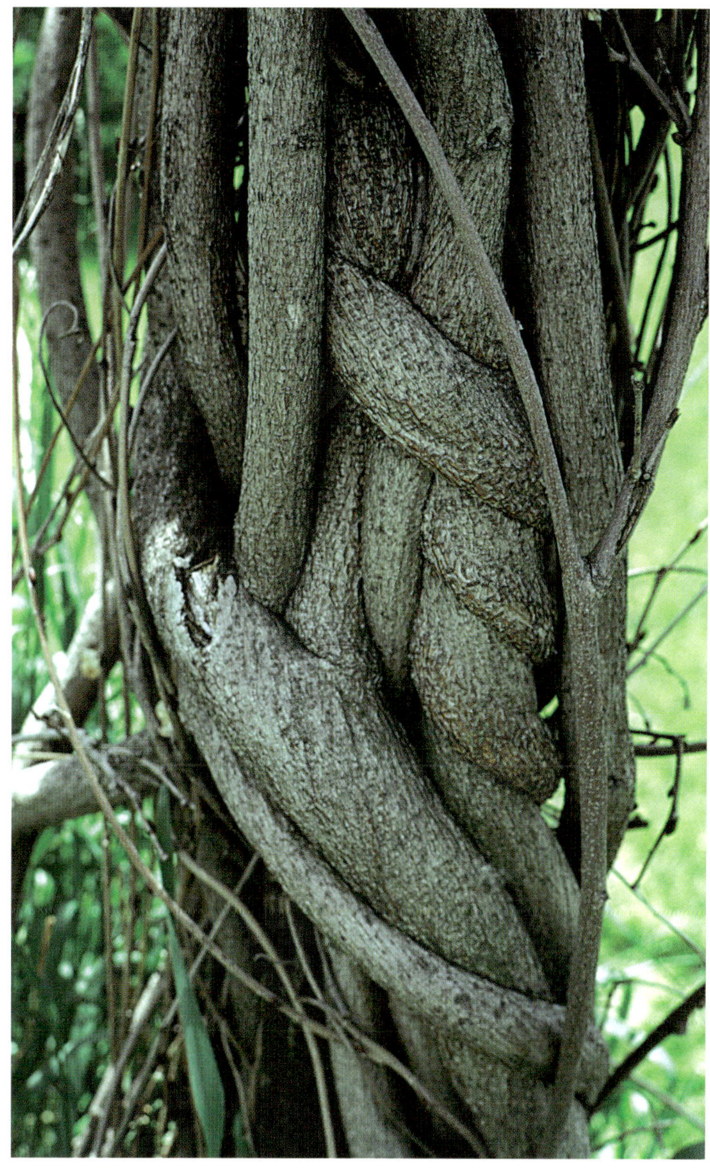

power out
in the night — torrents
lashing the pines

crossing linoleum
continents — an ant
stops at my foot

in ink-dark night
resting my paddles to drift
on floating stars

my tire flat
the holsteins calmly
turn to look

village cemetery
in the rain — someone
under a black umbrella

creak of wicker
from a screened porch
village dusk

through buzzing flies
the heifer's
steady gaze

dress clinging
sandals in hand — I walked
through the warm rain home

resting
on my shovel
a swallowtail

louder now
through the oldgrowth — buzz
of a chainsaw

on my back in the grass
for the cloud parade —
every beast of myth

chores in rose twilight
the quiet
jostle of sheep

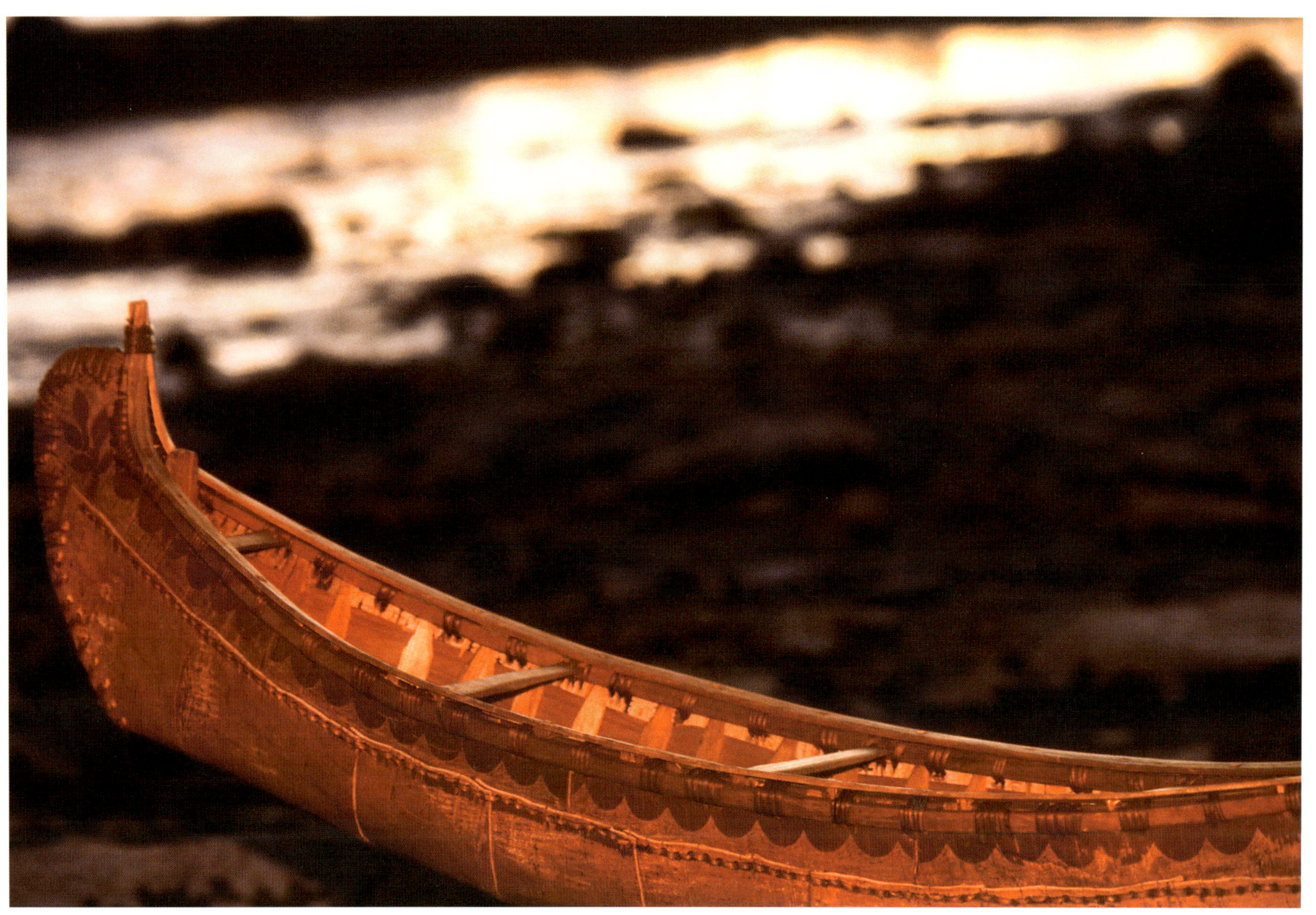

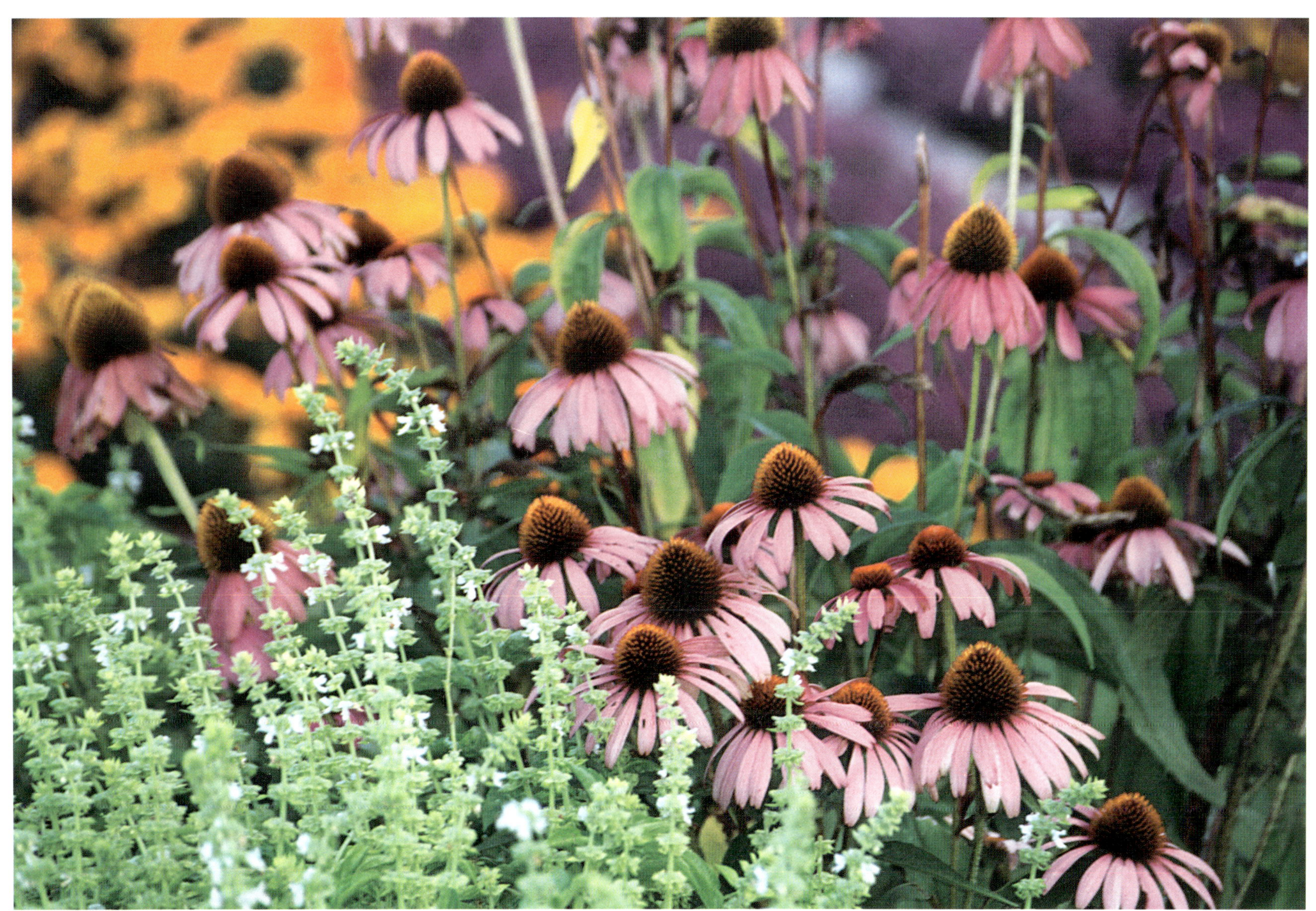

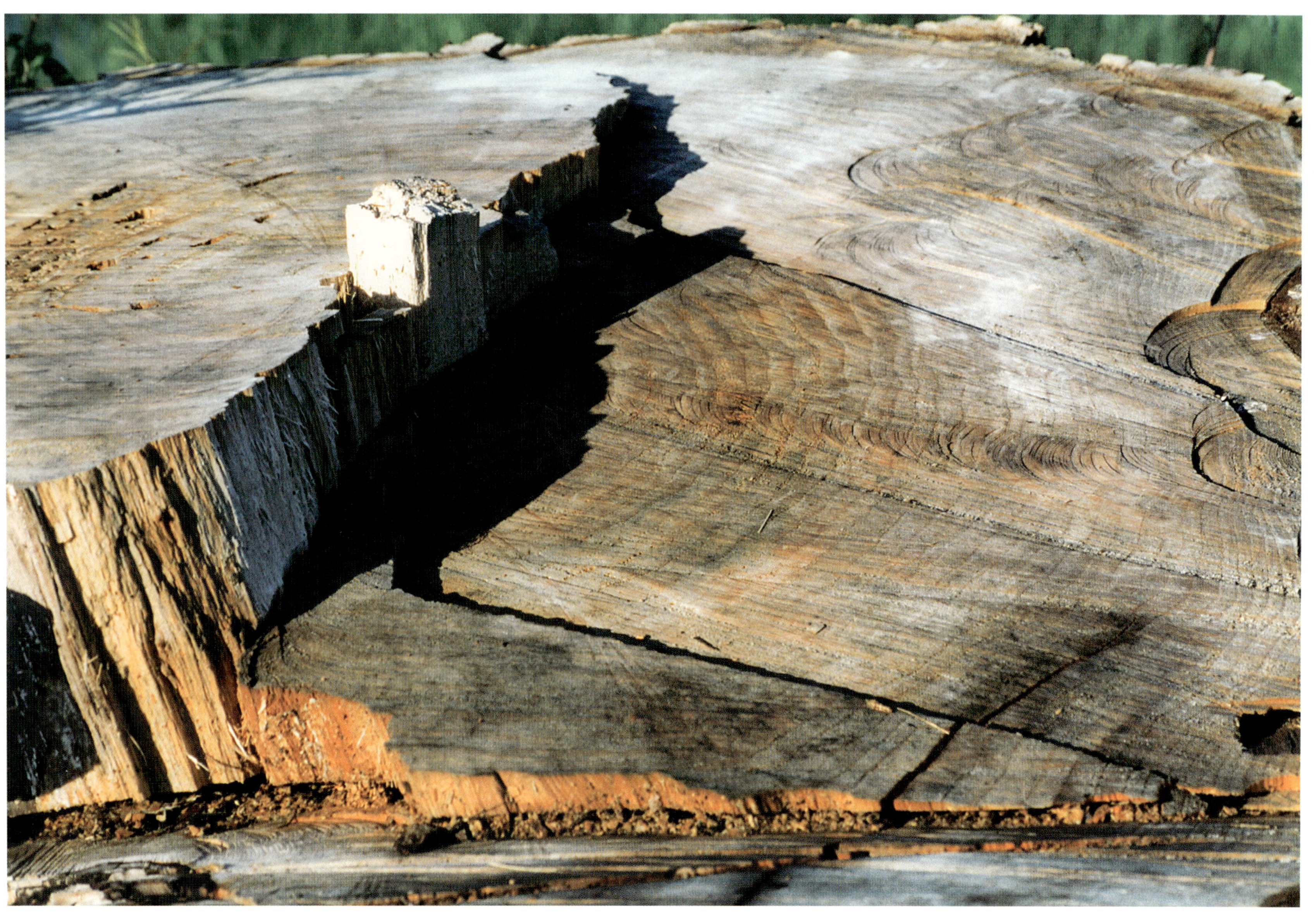

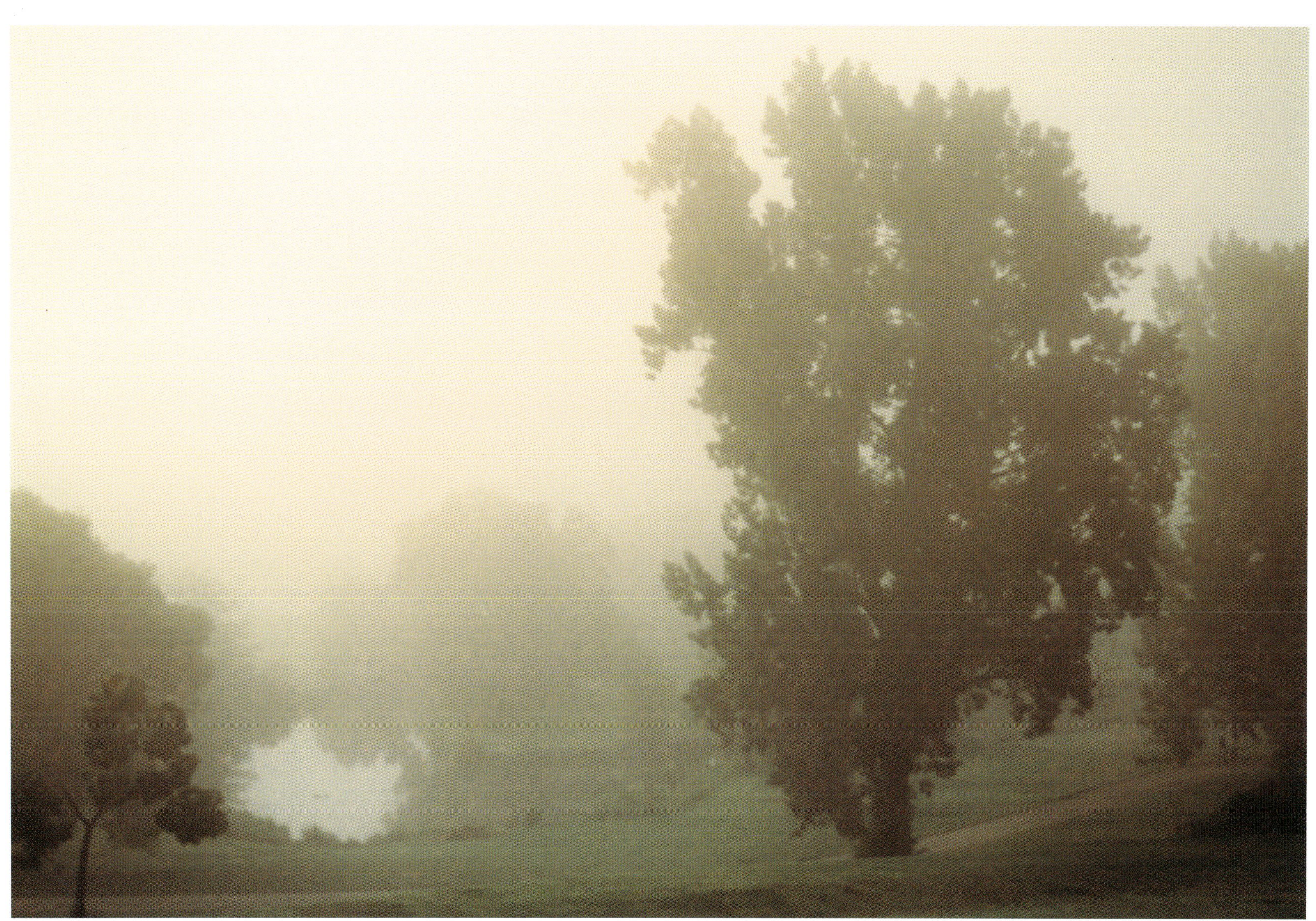

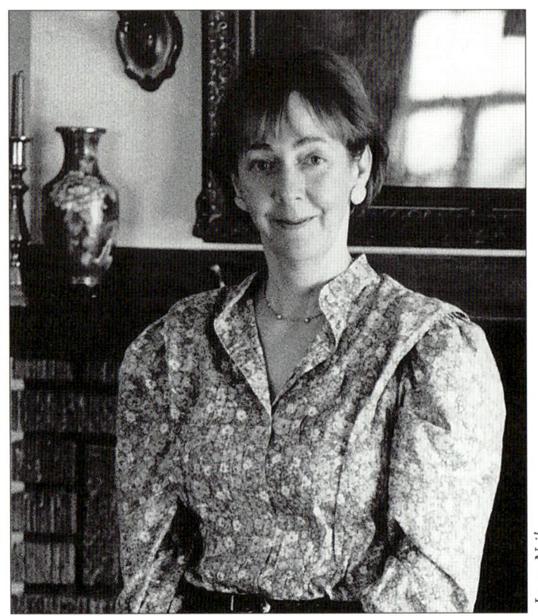

Larry Neily

Highly innovative in her work, MARIANNE BLUGER is a lyric poet with many books to her credit. A Christian with a firm grounding in Zen Buddhist meditation practice, she writes with the clarity of heart and mind that is a blessing common to both traditions. Of Bluger's earlier work, Judith Fitzgerald has written, "Whether she examines natural phenomena or illuminates human nature, it is abundantly clear that a powerful sensibility is at work in these poems."

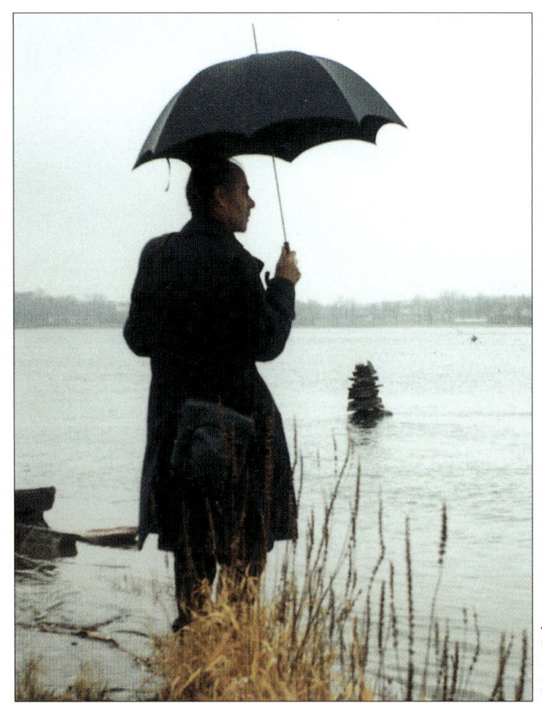

Maisa Lilja

David Suzuki has called RUDI HAAS, "an artist with a magical touch . . . a genius." Haas has produced many works in film, books, animated shorts, etc. and collaborated extensively on projects with Native Peoples in both Canada and Africa. He has received numerous honours, including the Art Directors Gold Medal Award.

We wish to credit the following artists:

Page 35
Charles Daudelin
"Untitled Bronze" 9'8 x 24'4 x 8'3
Collection: Department of Public Works
at the National Art Centre.

Page 41
Guido Molinari
"Homage to Samuel Beckett"
4 rectangular structures,
urethane on stainless steel
each 120 x 30 x 30 inches
Created for the 1967 exhibition, Toronto. First installed in Confederation Park, Ottawa, in 1969. Now at the National Gallery of Canada.

Page 57
Pierre Hardy, Daniel Riel,
Hubert Massé
Wall painting (mur mure '85 paix 2)
rue Eddy, Hull, Québec.

Page 64
John Seprano,
Temporary sculpture
Ottawa River near Parkdale Avenue.

Page 65
William McElcheran, 1976
"Untitled Bronze" 4'6 x 9'6 x 9"
Collection: Departmant of Public Works
Corner St. Andrew Street and Sussex Drive.

Page 77
Almuth Lütkenhaus-Lackey
"The Solstice" bronze, 2 metres diameter
Canadian Museum of Civilization.